FAITHS LO FOUND

FAITHS LOST AND FOUND

UNDERSTANDING APOSTASY

EDITED BY
MARTYN PERCY
AND CHARLES FOSTER

DARTON·LONGMAN+TODD

First published in 2023 by
Darton, Longman and Todd Ltd
1 Spencer Court
140 – 142 Wandsworth High Street
London SW18 4JJ

ISBN: 978-1-915412-32-4

A catalogue record for this book is available from the British Library.

Every effort has been made to trace the copyright owner of Norma Farber's
poem *Compassion*. The publisher would be glad to hear from the copyright
owner and due acknowledgement will be made in all future editions of the
book.

Printed and bound in Great Britain by Short Run Press, Exeter

Apostasy can take many forms. The cover of this book is Nicholas Mynheer's 'Mary Comforts Judas' Mother'. Although the gospels record no such encounter, the image reminds us that two mothers lost their sons on Good Friday to tragic and violent deaths. Mynheer, rather like the American poet Norma Farber (1909-1984) and her poem '*Compassion*', asks a question of us all:

> In Mary's house the mourners gather.
> Sorrow pierces them like a nail.
> Where's Mary herself meanwhile?
> Gone to comfort Judas's mother.

Contents

7

Contributors

The Editors

Professor Martyn Percy is the former Dean of Christ Church, University of Oxford. He is a member of the Faculty of Theology at the University of Oxford, and also tutors in the Social Sciences Division and the Said Business School. He is Professor of Theological Education at King's College London, and Visiting Professor at the Centre for the Study of Values, University of Winchester, and for the Centre of Theologically-Engaged Anthropology, University of Georgia. He is Patron of St Francis' Children's Society (an Adoption and Fostering Agency), Trustee of the Grubb Institute and the Li Tim-Oi Foundation, and a Vice-President of Modern Church.

He writes and teaches in two interrelated arenas: contemporary ecclesiology (specialising in Anglicanism, fundamentalism and new Christian movements); complemented, in turn, by writing on practical, pastoral and contextual theology, with significant work on Christianity and contemporary culture. His recent books include *Anglicanism: Confidence, Commitment, Communion* (Routledge), *Thirty-Nine New Articles: An Anglican Landscape of Faith* (Canterbury Press) and *The Futures of Anglicanism: Contours, Currents, Charts* (Routledge) and the *Oxford Handbook of Anglican Studies* (OUP, edited). His devotional writings include *Darkness Yielding*, *The Bright Field* and *Untamed Gospel* (all Canterbury Press). His work is now the subject of a book, *Reasonable Radical?: Engaging with the Writings of Martyn Percy* (Pickwick Publications/Wipf & Stock, 2018; Ed. Ian Markham).

Professor Charles Foster is a Fellow of Exeter College, University of Oxford, a member of the Oxford Law Faculty, a practising barrister and part-time judge, and the author of many books, including the New York Times Bestseller *Being a Beast* (Profile), *Being a Human* (Profile), *The Sacred Journey* (Thomas Nelson), *Wired for God: The Biology of Spiritual Experience* (Hodder), *The Selfless Gene: Living with God and Darwin* (Hodder), *The Jesus Inquest* (Lion Hudson), *The Christmas Story* (Authentic), and *Tracking the Ark of the Covenant* (Lion Hudson). A complete list of publications is at www.charlesfoster.co.uk/publications

He is himself a convert from conservative evangelical Christianity (he was an 'officer' at the notorious Iwerne camps) to Eastern Orthodoxy (via a long and winding road).

The authors of the case studies

Anthony Bash is Honorary Professor in the Department of Theology and Religion, Durham University.

Richard Baxter is Pastor for Outreach, Cary Baptist Church, Reading.

Tom Bohache is a U.S.-born author and independent scholar, who has published in the areas of queer biblical interpretation and theology. He is a retired seminary teacher and pastor.

Contributors

Janet Fife was one of the first women to be ordained in the Church of England. She is retired and lives in Whitby with her two dogs.

Rosie Harper is Chaplain to the Bishop of Buckingham and a Trustee of the Ozanne Foundation.

Nicholas Harris worked as a priest in the Church of England in Cumbria and London before leaving full time ministry to study art in Eastbourne and Chichester. Experiencing two nervous breakdowns in his middle years, he found stability through studying and teaching yoga and meditation. He continues to search after a kind and gentle spiritual path.

Ian S. Markham is the Dean and President of Virginia Theological Seminary.

Rosemary Sempell is an Archivist and Librarian in Australia.

Dan Warnke is a priest in the Church of England, chaplain of Westminster School and priest vicar of Westminster Abbey. He is currently a doctoral student at the University of Oxford, focusing on Christianity and contemporary culture, modern ecclesiology, and practical theology. He served as a church-planter in Vineyard Churches UK and Ireland from 2005 to 2016.

Introduction

Martyn Percy and Charles Foster

What does it cost a person to renounce the faith of their family, upbringing, peers or group, and then embrace another faith? For many who make this journey, the consequences can be traumatic and life-changing. They may be shunned by friends and family. Others are actively condemned, or regarded as 'dead' to the 'true faith'. Sometimes their lives may be in jeopardy.

These days, at least in the westernised world, loss of life is rare for those who abandon their original religious convictions. However, even in the twenty-first century, and within some branches of Christianity, 'apostasy' is regarded as an unforgiveable sin. For a person to embrace a new expression of belief is sometimes regarded as far worse than becoming an agnostic or even an atheist.

Studies of contemporary apostasy are pretty rare, though some are listed below. In a world where the religious economy is shaped by consumerism and individualism, and people are free to choose, blend and change their beliefs, it is increasingly hard to find orthodoxy at all, let alone to be troubled by people who switch their religion. The religious consumerism of the late twentieth and early twenty-first century is sometimes referred to as 'Sheilaism' – a shorthand term for an individual's system of religious belief which co-opts strands of multiple spiritual sentiments, religious ideas and artefacts, and sacred traditions. These are assembled as a kind of postmodern bricolage – one chosen by the individual – rarely involving theological considerations, and often lacking coherence .

The term 'Sheilaism' derived from a woman named Sheila Larson, who is quoted in the classic study *Habits of the Heart* (1985) by Robert Bellah and his colleagues. All Sheila does is follow her own inner 'little voice' in a faith she christens 'Sheilaism'. *Habits of the Heart* charts how North American faith, spirituality and religion have moved from being broadly public and unified to become largely private and personal concerns. This individualist and consumerist diversity means that America has around 400 million religions: everyone has their own personal faith. Diversity rules, and unity around orthodoxy rapidly evaporates under the intense heat of consumerism.

To demonstrate this seismic cultural shift, Bellah and his co-author colleagues quote a young nurse whom they name Sheila Larson:

'I believe in God. I'm not a religious fanatic. I can't remember the last time I went to church. My faith has carried me a long way. It's Sheilaism. Just my own little voice … It's just try to love yourself and be gentle with yourself. You know, I guess, take care of each other. I think He would want us to take care of each other' (R. Bellah, R. Madsen, W. Sullivan, A. Swidler & S. Tipton. (1985), *Habits of the Heart: Individualism and Commitment in American Life*, Berkeley, CA: University of California Press, p. 221).

If 'Sheilaism' is all there is, apostasy is not a relevant category.

So on the face of it, an exploration of apostasy might sound

Introduction

like an exploration of ancient history. Yet it is not. This book is an exploration of an important and troubling phenomenon which – because shifts between traditions are increasingly common – is increasingly important. It charts trauma, abuse, loss, pain, isolation and denigration.

We seek here to probe the social, psychological and theological dynamics of apostasy, and through personal, theological and spiritual reflection, examine the conditions and causes that prompt individuals to renounce one faith and embrace another. The term 'apostasy' (from the Greek, meaning defection or revolt), is the formal disaffiliation from, abandonment of, or renunciation of a religion by a person. It may also be defined more broadly as embracing an opinion that is contrary to one's previous religious beliefs.

The person who embarks on (let alone *commits!*) apostasy is known as an apostate. The term *apostasy* is used by sociologists to mean a divorce from *and* criticism of, or opposition to, a person's former religion, in a technical sense, with no pejorative connotation. Few former believers call themselves apostates, due to the term's negative connotation. Many religious groups punish apostates, and even if this is not officially sanctioned (as it may be, by, for instance, an edict of excommunication), conduct towards apostates may include cold-shouldering, verbal abuse and physical violence.

In this book we focus on the stories and testimonies of those who have left one iteration of Christianity and found themselves ostracised or banished by the community they have left, and yet have found a new spiritual home that has fostered and nourished their life, love and faith. We trace the journeys these people have taken, and learn what they have lost and found in the course of these (often traumatic) transitions.

We hear directly from individuals who have undertaken this

journey of faith. We offer some biblical, sociological, pastoral and cultural commentary on the narratives, helping the reader to navigate the issues of concern, as well as the sources of hope. Our primary concern is with the experiences of perceived apostasy in contemporary Christian belief and practice, and what they signify for individuals, groups and the public understanding of and regard for Christianity.

Traditionally, the Christian understanding of apostasy is 'a wilful falling away from, or rebellion against, Christian truth'. Conventionally, Christians have recognised four kinds of apostasy:

1. 'Rebellion': used to denote a coup or defection. This may involve schism.

2. 'Turning away from the Lord': idolatry or following false gods.

3. 'Falling away': distraction with material wealth or other non-essentials.

4. 'Adultery': unfaithfulness, and like literal adultery, blinded by lust or infatuation and unruly passions.

'Backsliding' is also a term commonly used within Reformed Evangelical Conservative Christianity (e.g. Christian Unions, certain kinds of House Church, Brethren, etc.) to describe an individual who converted to the relevant type of conservative Christianity but then reverts to pre-conversion habits, and/or lapses or falls into sin, or (which is regarded as itself falling into sin) finds a new spiritual home with a different kind of church or Christian faith. Such a person may find themselves labelled as deviant, regarded as 'lost', described as 'other', and therefore

16

shunned (and perhaps not even spoken of again).

The American sociologist Lewis A. Coser defined an apostate as not just a person who experienced a dramatic change in conviction but, someone who, 'even in [their] new state of belief, is spiritually living not primarily in the content of that faith, in the pursuit of goals appropriate to it, but only in the struggle against the old faith and for the sake of its negation'. The American sociologist David G. Bromley distinguished apostates from defectors and whistle-blowers as follows:

1. *Apostate*: occurs in a highly polarised situation in which an organisation member undertakes a total change of loyalties by allying with one or more elements of an oppositional coalition without the consent or control of the organisation.

2. *Defector*: the participant may negotiate their exit primarily with organisational authorities, who grant permission for the relinquishing of roles, control the exit process and facilitate role transmission (e.g., when marrying an outsider).

3. *Whistle-blower*: when an organisation member forms an alliance with an external regulatory agency through personal testimony concerning specific, contested organisational practices that the external unit uses to sanction the group/church.

Stuart A. Wright, another American sociologist, argued that apostasy is a distinct type of religious defection in which the apostate is a defector who is 'aligned with an oppositional coalition in an effort to broaden the dispute, and embraces public claims-making activities to attack his or her former group'. Bryan R. Wilson argued that apostates of new religious movements are generally in need of self-justification, seeking to reconstruct their past and to excuse their former affiliations, while blaming those who were formerly their closest associates.

We know of no other book that takes anything like our approach to the issue of apostasy. There are many books dealing with the issue – but all, so far as we can see, are stern injunctions not to engage in apostasy. They typically come from and are directed to conservative Protestant constituencies. Examples include John Owen and R. J. K. Law's *Apostasy from the Gospel* (Banner of Truth, 2021); James Barker's *Apostasy from the Divine Church* (Bookcraft, 1984); R. Dawson Barlow's *The Apostasy of the Christian Church* (Seedsower, 2014); O. Talmadge Spence's *Charismatism: Awakening or apostasy?* (Bob Jones University Press, 1978); Jeff Klutz's *Apostasy! The Word-Faith Doctrinal Deception* (ReturningKing.com, 2012) and Alexander Morrison's *Turning from Truth: A New Look at the Great Apostasy* (Deseret Books, 2010). We are well aware that these books, and many like them, are related to the concerns and constraints represented in their respective traditions. We are also mindful that this genre of literature rests on a kind of threat-reward axis. True believers are rewarded for loyalty. Apostates are, by definition, dissenters and deviant, and must be shunned and punished.

Faiths Lost and Found dwells on the trials and tribulations – and in some cases, the real terrors – that an apostate can experience as they move into a different spiritual home that nourishes their religious life, affirms their belief, and offers faith, hope and love. The book takes the reader on some deeply personal and traumatic faith-journeys, yet also offers accounts of resilience, faithfulness and profound fortitude. We hope and trust you will be challenged, inspired and encouraged in equal measure.

Limits and Elasticity: Finding the fringe of the Vineyard

Dan Warnke

It was in the late 1990s when a friend of mine at university first told me about a church called the 'Vineyard'. It made no sense to me, particularly as I was a new Christian with no background or upbringing in the church, so everything seemed disorientating. She spoke about it being a 'new' kind of church. I asked her what she meant because I thought the church was quite old, with stone buildings and spires; surely this was not something that you woke up one day and decided to 'start'? She spoke about her older brother, who was part of a group with a vision and passion for sharing God's love and serving the poor. Their idea was that faith should do something in your life. They sounded like the most unique and special sorts of people if they had 'permission' to start such a venture. These were the kind of people I wanted to meet. I knew nothing of doctrine, denominations, polity, ecclesiology, or the prevalent proclivities between faith communities. I was naive and curious, but I knew that this was something I should see for myself.

Faiths Lost and Found

With only one bus an hour, my arrival 'to church' was somewhat in advance of the indications necessary to make sense of a football stadium as a place of worship. I thought I was looking for a church, but this was not like any church I knew. There was no stone or spire, no stained-glass windows, gravestones, or railings. I had no idea if I was in the right place, but an open door leading to an upper-function room seemed the best bet. Ascending the stairs, I entered a large function room that carried the scent of the night before, confirmed by the sight of a bar lined with empty beer glasses. Numerous cables lay strewn across the floor, snaking between sound amps and instruments, giving the impression that I had either just walked into the aftermath of last night's gig or the set up for one to come. Across the vast corporate-tiled carpeted floor was a drum kit that sat centre-stage on a low platform, surrounded by numerous electric guitars and microphones, with what appeared to be 'roadies' busying themselves in purposeful activity. They were plugging things in and moving from one piece of equipment to the next with the sort of intensity that showed they meant business. The atmosphere was warm and friendly; people were chatting and happy as they set out chairs, leaflets, and a welcome desk alongside a table reserved for what looked like a mountain of doughnuts and gallons of coffee in anticipation of the masses. The sea of chairs, rows upon rows, would soon be filled with an enthused congregation of willing worshippers. This was no ordinary church gathering.

As a new Christian, I had taken it upon myself to visit every type of church I could find in my university town, but none had been like this. This was different. The atmosphere was electric and effervescent. The musicians took their places, amps were turned up, and the live music began in tones of 'soft rock' that inaugurated the 'soft start' of the service, confirming that you were indeed at the right 'gig'. I had no idea when it would all end or what was about to happen, but the lyrics and collective singing connected emotions and narrated an intimacy of Jesus as both a friend and redeemer. It was compelling. By the time the music ended, the seating had gone from half to mostly full as students and young families drifted into their places. This was 'Vineyard time'. Words of welcome and ways to be involved were shared from the front as the transition to the sermon took the shape of a short break with the abundance of doughnuts and coffee, allowing you time to 'get to know your neighbour'.

The married couple leading (the 'senior pastors'), were dressed casually and were warm, animated and spoke in the sort of formula now characteristic of a 'TED talk'. It was personal but informative, with real-life examples and relevance to contemporary life. Theirs was a faith that operated in the here and now, yet with the anticipation of 'more' to come.

The service eventually came to what seemed to be the end with an invitation to receive prayer in the would-be 'mosh pit', a space allocated between the front row and the staged area at the front. The mood was responsive and expectant as many in the congregation willingly navigated their way out of their row and towards the front in response to the various 'prophetic words' spontaneously being spoken by the senior leaders and by various trusted members of the congregation. However, this was not 'the end', but rather, it was articulated as the end of the 'formal part' of the service. This was something called 'ministry time'. It was all quite a sight as people pressed forward to those at the front who would place a hand on them to pray. People fell to the floor, others made strange sounds, and some seemed to be having what looked like colonic seizures. The sounds and movements were vast and varied, yet the atmosphere remained caring and kind as the band played melodic riffs from their earlier 'set list' as a sort of soundtrack to this apocalyptic scene. Throughout, the senior leaders calmly narrated all that was happening in a matter-of-fact style that reified the characteristically unusual human behaviour as being normative of 'the Kingdom' [of God].

I sat there, not knowing what to do, watching the whole spectacle and wondering if it was now time to leave. A kind person in the row in front noticed me looking a bit lost and turned to ask if this was my first time. I said I didn't know what to expect and asked if all that was happening was normal. 'Welcome to the Vineyard!' came the reply. We talked some more, and he asked if I wanted to join his group that met during the week to find out more. I was intrigued, so I agreed.

I continued to return each week and slowly made friends and grew in my faith. I never officially 'joined' the church (aside from giving my details for the church directory); there was no formal sign-up; you just sort of turned up and hung out. Membership (belonging) was framed within the three-fold criteria: gather on Sundays, join a weekly 'home group', and give financially. It seemed like the more you did, the more you belonged. At the time, I had no idea the reach and impact this first encounter would have and how it would fuel and frame everything that would follow.

Several years passed, and I moved back home to London, but it was still the early days of the Vineyard in the UK and Ireland, and only eleven existed. The nearest Vineyard church to where I lived was on the opposite side of London in Putney, and so when the rumour of one being planted nearby arose, I jumped at the chance of being involved. In my mid-twenties and newly married, I got stuck into the early phase of church-planting, and within a year or two, was being 'fast-tracked' through the leadership programme, invited to speak at conferences and participate in conversations about church growth. I had no formal training, but by my late twenties was leading a church-plant along with my wife and was seen as someone 'going places'. The church grew, people came to faith, we served the poor and were involved in the community in various ways, with many young people joining us as they looked for a place to call home, a church to belong to, and a people to call friends. It replicated much of the Vineyard in a stadium that I had first encountered (although we met in a cinema), and things seemed great.

The church was an eclectic, creative community with artists, actors, and those in the City. Some older, some younger, but mostly comprised of young professionals in their 20s and 30s with a few young children and babies in tow. Being in London meant we had people from all over the world; some were starting out in their careers, and others were passing through. Sometimes it felt like a train platform as an entire carriage of passengers arrived and another left. The footfall was high, and only a small core ever remained. No one minded, but the emotional drain of constantly making new friends, helping people move home, and throwing parties so frequently that your house is just a carousel of food and conversations did take its toll. But this was much of what the Vineyard was about, genuinely being in each other's lives and looking out for anyone who needed help. Prayer, prophesying, serving the poor and worship all served as a response to the love of God, an expression of the Kingdom in our midst. All this effervescence was held together through the language of 'vision and values' that focussed our activities and shaped the virtue of participation. Within this narrative thrust, church membership was framed within *social set theory*, specifically a 'centred-set' model (the other two being 'bounded-set' and 'fuzzy-set'), that located belonging as something of a dynamic movement towards the centre of the set. Within this model, relationships with those orientated towards the centre become vital to the cohesion needed for the set to thrive. Or, to put it another way, a clearly articulated centre (vision) operates the conditions necessary for a growing church.

The metaphor often used to describe all this was a moth's attraction to light in a darkened room. The job of the senior pastors was to describe the light (vision) sufficiently for it to shine brightly in the darkness. Confusingly, this was also interchangeable with Jesus as the centre (light), leaving me wondering if the vision and Jesus were supposed to be one and the same. I had no formal theological training at this point, so all I could do was ask these sorts of questions and defer my misunderstandings. I still had questions, though.

The use of this 'centred-set' model also identified those close to the centre as having commitments that equate to greater leadership potential and deeper loyalties (stronger bonds). Conversely, whilst those further away from the centre were not regarded as being of 'lesser' value to the set, they were seen to possess little influence and *charismata* – which were seen as essential to evoking the presence of God's Kingdom reign (weaker bonds). The real issue, however, was less about concentric proximity to the centre (although the implicit was that being closer was better) and more about the direction and velocity of travel. Your trajectory was everything. If you were far away but travelling towards the centre, you were perceived to be attracted by the vision and likely to 'stick'. Conversely, those who had been part of the 'core' of the church – the centre of the set – significantly involved as members, yet were seemingly drifting away from the centre, were perceived as no longer following the 'vision'. They were left to their own devices, were no longer part of key decisions, and were kept in the dark. That, after all, was the direction they had chosen.

Ultimately it all came down to a simple idea: you were

either headed towards the centre of the set, or you were not. This was not framed as judgement but rather as a matter of fact; as a matter of choice. If the vision was clearly articulated, if the senior pastors had correctly discerned the work of God in that place, then you were (by definition) participating in the very activity of God's Kingdom, in the here and now. As a free agent, you could therefore choose to belong through your active participation. The main issue, then, was not how close you were to the centre, but your operant presence and direction of travel. Under these conditions, it was better to be far away (i.e. a seeker) travelling towards the centre (or vision), than it was to be close yet drifting away. It was the negative change of trajectory that became problematic.

As a church-planter I had experienced the centre, and I helped create the vision and focus necessary to sustain the centre. So, when my trajectory appeared to deviate, when I appeared to be travelling away, it was as if I had become apostatic. I had no idea what it would be like to be in and around the centre of the Vineyard, to be amongst the people making decisions and choices for the movement. The senior leadership are kind and compassionate, but they are focused and intense. Much like any nascent organisational structure, the Vineyard is an operation of sorts that necessitates a level of logistics and single-mindedness to build momentum. As a result, the theological temperament of the Vineyard is *cataphatic* in nature; all talk related to God and 'the Kingdom' is successful and positive. There is seemingly little energy for anything, or anyone, who questions this positivity or appears to be draining energy from the centre. At the centre, there is no room for the negative. This is compounded by the Vineyard being replete with aphorisms and idioms that compress organisational constructs into positive, pithy sayings. One such saying is, 'celebrate what you want to replicate'. This typically

25

meant sharing testimonies from the front of the church, or conference stage that would always conclude with some sort of a triumph – essentially, all is now as it should be. I had a problem with this idea: Jesus spoke about the weak and the poor always being with us, so surely an authentic narrative would also, at times, involve failure. Consequentially, that meant weakness could only be shared if the testimony concluded with victory (the person was healed, the church grew, and things are now better). Ultimately, success stories were the only stories.

I continued to ask questions about ecclesiology which only seemed to be met with caution. I remember during one Vineyard UK leadership workshop, asking a member of the senior leadership about the limits and elasticity of Vineyard ecclesiology (particularly, given that I was now planting a church on a council estate – not the norm for the Vineyard), only to be met with the response: 'I think you should just focus on growing the church.' It seemed that unless the church I led was around 200-300 strong, my curiosity and enquiry were wasted efforts. And even then, the next question that I should be asking was: 'How do I now grow the church to 500?' Those were the right questions to ask, but those were not the questions *I* needed to ask. Looking back, I can now see that the trajectory that brought me into the Vineyard was not the one that would have me land in the centre, but rather, beyond. In this way, my questions took on something of an *apophatic* nature, moving beyond the language of Set Theory and vision statements, and way outside the bandwidth of Vineyard ecclesiology. In short, my questions seemed to gravitate towards the negative spaces of what was missing in the Vineyard. I was curious about the spaces that a language of success simply could not name. Through this line of enquiry, my experience went from enjoying close contact with much of the Senior leadership for over a decade, to slowly finding myself in total silence. My questions had led me to the edge, and finally to the outside. Unknowingly, I had reached the limit of the concentric rings repeating the centre of the set. It felt lonely.

A further one of these aphorisms, or 'Wimberisms' (so named after the founder of the Vineyard, John Wimber), often cited during Vineyard conferences was that the church should 'keep its back door as large and open as the front door – the primary goal is to lengthen the distance between the two.' People will come and go, but the activities of the church should keep them engaged for as long as possible. Whilst this temporal approach is true of our earthly existence, it draws heavily on the model of a market economy, rather than one of grace. Or, to put it another way, the sentiment concedes that the church should 'let the market decide'. The result of this is that the church can, unintentionally, become utilitarian and operant in nature, focusing on the effectiveness of those tasked with lengthening the distance between the axiomatic 'front' and 'back' doors. Consequently, if the church is not growing, the diagnosis is that the distance between the two has not been sufficiently lengthened and/or there are not enough people entering through the front (the work of evangelism). No one is, therefore, particularly concerned with those heading out the 'back door', and as such, they seemingly find their exit is silent. I was eventually going to learn this first-hand.

I had thought that I was committed; I had thought that I was on a continuum toward the centre of the set; but the centre did not see it that way. As a young couple, my wife and I had ventured out on this church-planting journey together. All we really knew was couples' ministry. Every member of the senior leadership was married, and as the senior pastors, the husband and wife team formed the prototype for any would-be church-planters. It was your unity and partnership in the Gospel that would help to share the vision and build the church. Your marriage witnessed to the life of Christ and the fidelity of his church. So, it came as a significant change of gear when my wife concluded, after several years of being one-half of this team, that this 'church-planting business' was not for her. Her vocation lay elsewhere. But given the dominance of this couples' ministry model, it was not an easy adjustment to make within the ecology of the wider movement. Whilst this decision was accepted by the upper echelons of Vineyard leadership, it was not received well. How could I remain committed if my wife no longer was? Active participation and commitment were consummate. Looking back, this was the first of many changes that would eventually lead to my departure and my experience of the proverbial back door.

Once I had become the 'single' church-planter — my wife now happily pursuing her own career — I started to be treated differently. It was as if I had deviated from the 'right' way of doing church. This manifested itself in the smallest of ways as if I had been 'dropped from the squad'. I began asking questions. Many questions. I was vocal and keen to discuss and debate ideas on church-planting, growth models, and Vineyard ecclesiology. I wanted to become more engaged with faith in the public square and explore how our theology informed the way that we engaged in the world. However, as I discovered, my questions could only stretch so far before I soon found myself tracing the margins of the set and perceived as one heading away from the centre. During this time I started using liturgy and shaping Sunday worship around the centrality of the Eucharist. As far as I was concerned, I was trying to extend the charismatic-evangelical tradition of the Vineyard, but these developments were seen as odd, religious elements of the established church that posed a stumbling block to growth. People were not interested in religion, I was told; they just needed a fresh encounter with God. I once asked a member of the senior leadership team at a national conference why we did not offer Holy Communion as a way of bringing everyone together, but was soon rebuffed, as it was 'simply not practical'. I replied that I thought it was the only thing that really held us all together. This was not received well, as if I was clearly not getting what it was all about. It seems that apostasy was perceived in my trajectory before it became a reality.

My curiosity drove an appetite for further study, and so after an MA in theology and politics at King's College London, and then further study in Oxford, the writing was beginning to appear on the wall. Studying the concrete realities of the church revealed that the Vineyard was one node of connection rather than the destination and centre of my faith. As I began questioning this further, it became an exploration of the Anglican communion and a call to priesthood in the Church of England. My convictions grew deeper, and with it, the breadth of my ecclesial horizon and the catholicity of the church. To my surprise, I found a more radical catholicity deep within my faith that was starting to surface. I suspect it was always there, but the things I was beginning to want to do in my own church were simply not part of the 'Vineyard DNA'. I had no intention of breaking away or causing difficulty, so I took this to the people of my church and explained that it seemed I needed to leave. They were characteristically kind and supportive, and it was a huge relief. I then took this to the senior leadership of the Vineyard. That was a different story. Within days it set in motion a mechanism of phone calls and meetings that felt like I was being squeezed out as quickly as possible. It was as if I had become an anathema, excommunicated, put out in the cold. I was a problem to solve, a ticking bomb to neutralise, a resource that needed managing. To say it was challenging was an understatement. I loved the people of the church, and it was already painful to say goodbye, so to be treated as if I had done something wrong was hard to bear. I experienced the power, and control of the centre as my voice became lost in the din of quasi-managerial speak that carried the implicit understanding that this was all 'pleasing to the Lord'. Before leaving, I was asked to give the church space, not to communicate with anyone in the church, to avoid undermining the nascent loyalties yet to be established with the new senior leaders.

At the point of my eventual departure, I wrote a letter of thanks to the National Directors – to this day, I remain grateful for my time in the Vineyard – and received a kind reply. But then, it was as if the tap was turned off. I heard nothing; no one has ever contacted me since. I do not exist.

Apostasy or Adherence? Roman Catholic to Evangelical

Richard Baxter

My name is Richard Baxter. Neither my committed Catholic mum nor my atheist dad knew they were giving me the same name as the seventeenth-century Puritan minister who wrote *The Reformed Pastor*. Nor do I think either expected me to become a pastor in a conservative evangelical church, leading to me hearing a fair number of quite predictable jokes around my name, theological position, and role in the church.

What my parents did do, however, was love me. My upbringing in suburban, middle-class south-east England wasn't perfect but it was comfortable, and I was part of a family in which I wasn't only loved, but in which I *knew* I was loved. Not because of my achievements or obedience, but unconditionally. I don't take that blessing for granted.

In my story I'll speak of a number of blessings of my birth and upbringing, one of which is this: In a book on apostasy, I may be the only person who, to my knowledge, has never been called an apostate – either by my family, or by St Joseph's, the church I grew up in. There were points of tension of course, and there remain hugely important disagreements between the beliefs I held growing up, and the faith I now hold. But I never felt rejected by my family, or indeed by Father Bill from St Joseph's, who asked me several times in the years after my conversion what would bring me back into the fold.

Like many children growing up going to church, I found services not only boring but, because we attended the Sunday p.m. Mass weekly, a signal for me the end of the weekend, and the beginning of another week of school. However, I continued to go with my mum and older brother and, at age fourteen, I was confirmed. Unlike many of my peers who received confirmation and then quickly stopped attending church regularly, I continued to attend and in fact began to enjoy going to church. As a fairly uncool teenage lad at an all-boys school, church was pretty much the only place where I got to talk (awkwardly) to girls, and I can't pretend that wasn't part of the new appeal of Mass. I like to think it did go a little deeper than that though!

Although my dad was a convinced atheist, I don't remember him ever trying to convince me or my brother of this position and I'm not sure I even realised he was an atheist until my late teens (he used to come with us to church two or three times a year). Perhaps partly because of this, I had always considered belief in God natural, and I can't think of a time when I didn't believe in God. Around my confirmation though, I began to take belief in God more seriously. Indeed, I was convinced that Jesus is the Son of God who lived, died, and rose again three days later. I even wore a crucifix, perhaps to remind myself of this faith and also to indicate this belief to others.

While I had always gone to Mass, I now went because I wanted to, and continued to be an altar server until around seventeen years of age. At one point in my teenage years, I even served for Cormac Murphy-O'Connor, at that point Bishop of

Arundel and Brighton, and later Cardinal of Westminster.

This was where I was at in terms of faith until I went away to university in mid-Wales — taking my faith seriously, as far as I understood it. Straight away, I began to attend St Winifred's Catholic Church, and soon discovered that the early Saturday evening service was preferable since it meant one didn't need to attend hungover the next morning. As well as St Winifred's, I regularly attended the University Christian Union (CU) on a Friday evening. Why not? After all, I was a Christian, wasn't I? The only context in which I knew about Catholics and Protestants was Northern Ireland — and I didn't think that had anything to do with difference of belief; only politics and power. As for 'evangelical', that wouldn't have been a term I'd ever heard, and if anyone ever told me they were born again I would likely have assumed they were telling me they were American. The Christians at the CU were a bit weird. They didn't get drunk and didn't swear. But they were nice, too; very welcoming and friendly. I can remember one gently challenging me by telling me one time that he didn't believe the Pope is infallible — but I was able to assure him that I didn't either, so that was all okay!

The CU meetings must have been very different to the services I had grown up with — each week, a preacher would visit and a large part of the meeting was taken up with him explaining and applying a particular Bible passage. However, I don't remember finding the meetings strange, or remember hearing anything that challenged my thinking and belief. Looking back, I do believe the reality that Paul speaks of in 2 Corinthians 4 was at play: 'The god of this age [Satan] has blinded the minds of unbelievers, so that they cannot see the light of the gospel that displays the glory of Christ, who is the image of God.' A couple of months into university however, a particular CU meeting was deeply challenging to me. That evening the preacher was Michael, a man from Northern Ireland. He described his conversion from Roman Catholicism to Evangelical Protestantism, after losing both hands when the bomb he was constructing for a paramilitary group blew up under him. I have no idea what the passage he was meant to be speaking from was, but what I do remember was the way he said repeatedly about a number of different theological issues, 'The Roman Catholic Church says [x], but the Bible teaches [y]'. Michael's talk that evening felt like a sledgehammer to me. It was the first time I can ever remember wondering whether I was actually a Christian or not. As he spoke, I became angry that he could suggest I perhaps wasn't a Christian, but by the end I was anxious and upset, thinking, 'He keeps saying the Bible and my church aren't saying the same thing. But I've never read the Bible, so I have no idea if he's telling the truth.'

That evening, almost twenty-four years ago, I can remember talking to two people. First, I spoke to Jonathan who worked for the CU, and he suggested we read John's gospel together, so that I could explore what the Bible teaches. Second, I spoke to my mum from my hall of residence payphone (this was the late 1990s!). I'll say more about that conversation later.

Over the next couple of months, leading up towards the Christmas of my first year at university, Jonathan and I met up weekly to read and discuss sections of John's gospel. To begin with, my idea had been to work out exactly what Catholicism teaches, and what Protestantism teaches, and then to discern which fits with the Bible's teaching. Within a few weeks, I realised I wasn't clever enough for this, and that I simply needed to listen to what Jesus said. As I did so, I discovered that my understanding of God didn't always fit well with what the Bible teaches.

I had always thought that if I did this, this, and this good thing, God would be pleased with me, and accept me into heaven. However, as I read of Jesus telling us that 'anyone who sins is a slave to sin', I began to recognise that I couldn't do all those good things. This was deeply unpleasant. I'd always recognised that I'd done wrong, but I hadn't ever considered myself to be alienated from God, unable to come to him. However, I also discovered that God was far more like a loving parent than I had ever recognised. Just as my parents had loved me, not because of obedience or achievements but unconditionally, so the Father loved this world and gave his Son to live that perfect life I had failed to live, to die the death that would have been mine, and then to rise again to freely give new life to all who trust him.

There were two aspects of this that seemed new to me (I'm not claiming I had never heard them growing up, but I don't remember doing so).

First, despite wearing a crucifix for several years, previously my only understanding of the death of Christ had been that it was necessary for him to die, in order to rise again and prove that he was the Son of God. It was through reading John's gospel, as well as listening more carefully to the preaching at the CU, that I began to recognise the claim that Christ died 'for our sin' – to pay the debt that we couldn't. Of course, this far from exhausts the meaning of the cross, but it was at this time that I discovered this aspect for the first time.

Second, the grace of God. The freeness of forgiveness and acceptance was what really struck home, excited, and fascinated me – and continues to do so decades later.

My growing understanding of the gospel and growing awareness of my sin and alienation from God culminated in me crying out to God and trusting in Christ, in December 1998, as I walked up the hill to my hall of residence. At that point I felt an overwhelming sense of peace and I would say that it was then that I became a Christian. While it might be gentler to say I went from Catholic to evangelical, for me it was more fundamental than that. I went from not trusting Christ, to trusting him. I went from not believing the gospel, to believing it. I went from being under God's judgement, to being part of his family. I went from not being a Christian, to being a Christian.

Having told you my experience, I want to talk about some of the points of tension, and some blessings I recognise.

Many of those points of tension in my life in relation to religion and faith have been about recognising the seriousness of sin, resulting in separation from God, both for myself and for others. The most painful experiences haven't been due to interpersonal conflict or accusations of betraying my faith, but due to seeing the lostness of myself or of others. However, there have been points at which there has been, at the very least, awkwardness as a result of a move from Catholicism to evangelicalism. I'll mention the main ones I remember.

The night when Michael preached at the CU, and I was left in doubt as to whether I was a Christian, I rang my mum from the payphone. I told her something like, 'I'm not sure that I'm a Christian, and I'm not sure that the Catholic Church is Christian!' This was likely not the most helpful thing to have told her that evening, and she warned me to be careful in looking into matters of faith. I think her response was one primarily of concern – I was five hours away from home, perhaps being unduly influenced by a religious group who could very easily be a harmful and destructive cult. What parent wouldn't be worried?

Not long after that, when I was still exploring or had recently trusted Christ, I can remember an encounter with an English lad living on the same corridor as me. I would describe him as a lapsed Catholic – he hadn't been to Mass in the time we had been at university, but certainly retained the label. He told me that Protestants were dangerous, and that I really ought to keep my distance from the CU. I do find it interesting when I hear that evangelicals are considered a cult in parts of Europe, as I don't think this is utterly rare in the UK either.

There were Catholics who felt I was much too into reading and seeking to understand the Bible. I can remember great sadness when someone who I love very much wrecked my Bible, in an attempt to stop me reading it so much. I recollect the reason they gave was that in their view I wasn't adequately living according to its teachings, but stopping me reading those teachings seemed unlikely to help with that. Looking back, I'm surprised that I wasn't angry with them for destroying my property, but I was more sad that they would seem to hold the word of God with contempt in such a way. Another time, when chatting to people in the street about the gospel one evening, I can remember a drunk Catholic telling me that salvation by grace alone meant that being a Protestant is much easier than being a Catholic, because it means you can just live however you want to!

Along with the earliest time of exploration of faith traditions, being baptised as a believer was perhaps the greatest point of tension within my family. For my atheist dad, I think the move from one tradition to another and the desire to be baptised was simply bemusing. For my mum, since to her understanding I had been baptised as an infant, being baptised as a believer at age 21 seemed like a rejection of what I had been brought up with, and since religion, culture and family all tend to be intertwined with one another, this certainly brought some relational tension for a time. However, my mum, dad and brother all came along to my baptism, for which I am thankful both to God and to them.

One other point at which my dad found it hard to accept my choices in terms of living out my faith was when, a couple of years after completing university, I spent a voluntary year with the evangelical organisation London City Mission. The problem wasn't anything to do with theology or religion, just that spending a year at that point in my life doing voluntary work could easily stop me from embarking on a career as he would have liked to have seen me doing. My dad was not materialistic, but I don't think the choice made sense to him. Years later, he was very supportive of me beginning to work for a church, when he realised that was what my wife and I wanted to do long term.

While I've found hard words and misrepresentation from acquaintances fairly easy to shrug off, tension with family has landed much harder because they are the ones I love and who love me the most, and who know me the best. In reflecting on those points of tension, misunderstandings and so on, I consider that if my eyes were blinded, so are the eyes of those who might disagree with my move. I want them to know Christ and his free grace as well. Since my conversion took place soon after I went away to university, I was away from the church I had grown up in, and because from age 8 to 18 I had not attended a Catholic school, most of my peer group were not Catholic, and none of my closest friends were. This also would have meant that, while many of my friends might not have understood me changing my Christian tradition, they would have been unlikely to be against me doing so.

I'm so thankful that I had parents who dimly mirror God's parental love, and who disagreed with some of my decisions without rejecting me. I know others who have made journeys from Catholicism to evangelicalism or from other religions to Christianity who have been ostracised by family, and I am thankful that hasn't been my experience. I'd like to think evangelicals seeing loved ones move to another tradition, religion or lifestyle would manage to avoid rejecting them, but I'm certain there are many from an evangelical background with stories of being ostracised by family when moving away from that faith tradition. Specifically from my Catholic upbringing, I'm very thankful for two things in particular: a moral/ethical framework, and saying creeds every Sunday since the truths of those creeds came to life for me once I came to know Christ. These creeds gave me a framework for much vital Christian truth that many – including many churchgoing Christians – simply have not received.

The truths about our triune God that those ecumenical creeds contain brings me back to the term 'apostasy'. Not only have I not been called an apostate by others, I do not view myself as an apostate. In using the label 'evangelical' I don't see myself as cut off from all pre-eighteenth or sixteenth-century church history, but as a Christian who is seeking to be faithful to truths of Scripture that have been believed through all the centuries that Christ has been building his Church, from Pentecost to the present. The evangelical movement doesn't do this perfectly, and neither do I! However, I hope I do seek a right catholicity, with an emphasis on God's freely given grace, as made known in his Scriptures, that are not an apostasy from any true Christianity, but a fulfilment of it. I have been blessed by God in so many ways. With my family. With my upbringing. With my experience of conversion. With my wife and children. With my church family. But most of all, I am blessed by the free gift of his Son, to bring me freely into his family now and forever.

A Wideness in God's Mercy

Janet Fife

The evening I was confirmed was one of the loneliest of my life. I had left a tight-knit Evangelical Free Church, losing most of my social circle, and when I informed my staunchly Nonconformist parents that I was joining the Church of England they disowned me. The other confirmation candidates were surrounded by proud parents and godparents; I had no godparents and my parents weren't speaking to me. To cap it all, the bishop, Peter Ball – who had mingled with those surrounded by happy families – didn't speak to me at the reception after the service. I went home feeling very low, and wondering what on earth I had done.

My parents saw my defection to the Church of England as a betrayal of the sound Christian upbringing they had given me. My father, Eric Fife, had been an Evangelical Free Church pastor in Winchester and a disciple of the renowned Calvinist preacher Martyn Lloyd-Jones, before taking the family to the USA in 1955 to represent the North Africa Mission (NAM) there. Before long he left NAM to become Missionary Director of Inter-Varsity Christian Fellowship (IVCF; now InterVarsity), the American sister organisation to the British Inter-Varsity Fellowship (now UCCF). IVCF worked on university campuses across the USA and Canada. It was theologically conservative while maintaining a high intellectual standard, but its conservatism did not extend to social issues. IVCF employed its first full-time black staff worker in 1952, when racial segregation was still widely practised across the USA, and it encouraged women in Bible teaching roles from the early 1950s. These were among the features which distinguished conservative evangelicalism from fundamentalism in the USA.

My father's job involved visiting North American universities and mission fields across the world; he also ran a summer training camp for aspiring missionaries, and spoke at other camps and conferences across the USA and Canada. During the summer vacations we travelled with him, mingling with campers, IVCF staff members, and speakers. Sometimes, even as young children, we went to lectures. When at home we were often visited by Christian leaders from across the globe; we, in turn, visited the homes of Billy Graham and some of his team members. I grew up in the heart of American evangelicalism and imbibed its thinking and values. It was this heritage my parents felt I had betrayed by becoming an Anglican – but the rot had set in many years before.

When my father worked for IVCF we lived in the Chicago suburbs and attended a large Baptist church which had the distinction of having once been pastored by Billy Graham. Naturally, the church had a strong emphasis on evangelism and 'knowing Jesus Christ as your personal Saviour'. I was about 7 or 8 when my Sunday school teacher asked the class: 'Have you asked Jesus into your heart?' It seemed a good thing to do, so after going to bed that evening I duly asked Jesus into my heart. Nothing happened and I felt no different. A couple of Sundays later my teacher asked the question again. Disappointed with the lack of apparent result the first time of asking, I tried a different approach. I prayed, 'Lord, if you're real, show me.' At once I saw a vision of Jesus and his disciples, shining brighter than lightning. Satisfied this time, I asked God to make me good and went to sleep. I didn't talk about this experience – it didn't seem the kind of thing to be talked about.

Despite this rather mystical start to my devotional life, my faith didn't seem particularly personal during my childhood and early teens. No doubt this was partly because our dysfunctional family life (of which I have written elsewhere) had left me repressed and emotionally stunted. I was also becoming aware, as I grew older, that the commitment to Christ and personal relationship with Jesus that others so glibly talked of seemed sometimes to be only skin deep. Most of the children in my Sunday school class were able (unlike me) to lead the class in prayer at a moment's notice – but when the teacher was absent they discussed games of strip poker they had played.

I knew less about the private behaviour of the adults, of course, but in those who seemed genuinely committed there was often a narrowness and joylessness that was unattractive. The church members tended to be more conservative than the IVCF personnel. Many harmless activities were taboo: going to the movies, dancing, playing cards, drinking alcohol, listening to rock music, beards and long hair on men. My parents were more open, but worried about being condemned as 'unsound'. I remember my mother's nervousness when she took us to see *Mary Poppins,* lest we be seen by church people. IVCF expected staff to raise their own financial support: had we been seen breaking a taboo, a drop in donations would have been a likely result and we literally might go hungry. I grew up with an unhealthy fear of offending people which I battle with to this day.

The atmosphere of American suburban middle-class evangelicalism in the 1950s and 1960s was suffocating, while in youth culture generally the 1960s saw an explosion of creativity and freedom. For teenagers like us, the tension was enormous. Through the late 1960s and early 1970s, we became increasingly disillusioned with the Church. One afternoon when my parents were out, my sisters and I did the most sinful thing we could think of – we played cards for money. On a Sunday!

In my senior year of high school, as demonstrating students were shot dead on campus by National Guardsmen and it became clear that the Age of Aquarius had dawned stormy, we began to hear of a religious revival among young people. The Jesus Movement, as it was called, was largely linked to the burgeoning charismatic movement in which Christians of all ages were increasingly involved. My uncle Reg, who with Auntie Lily attended a large Pentecostal church in Philadelphia, had sent us a copy of John Sherrill's book *They Speak with Other Tongues*. The book gave the history of the charismatic movement from its beginnings in Pentecostalism until the time of writing in 1964, and it featured my uncle and aunt's church. I read it with considerable interest. At the same time we were hearing reports of hippies and other young people, with no previous connection with churches, walking into Sunday morning services wanting to find God. Sadly, those churches didn't always know how to respond, and sometimes focused more on the men's long hair and the women's miniskirts than in meeting the spiritual needs of their wearers. Nevertheless, something exciting was clearly going on, and I was intrigued.

I graduated from high school on 11 June 1971; on 21 June *Time* Magazine's lead story was 'The Jesus Revolution'. It explored the phenomenon of young people turning en masse to Christ; the cover picture was a psychedelic image of Jesus. I traced and re-coloured that image again and again. I was burning to know more about both the charismatic renewal and the Jesus Movement. We were living in Florida by then but were due to travel north and would be visiting Uncle Reg and Auntie Lily and their church in Philadelphia, the Tabernacle. Here was an opportunity to see for myself what was going on. I prepared by studying everything the Bible had to say about the Holy Spirit. The Bible study skills I had imbibed as a child, and my father's reference library, proved useful.

The Tabernacle was unlike any church I'd ever attended — and my experience by that time was pretty wide. I was used to services so dreary that I once complained, 'Why don't they call it Rainday, it's so depressing.' But the Tab, as it was called, was crowded, bursting with life, and full of joy. My sister Brenda and I then attended a midweek home group for young people. The group laid hands on us and prayed that we would be filled with the Holy Spirit. They expected us to speak in tongues, but nothing happened. They told us first to stand, then to sit, then kneel. When they told us to start praying in gibberish, I'd had enough. 'I've asked to receive the Holy Spirit,' I declared, 'and Jesus said God gives the Holy Spirit to those who ask. I believe I've received.' Then, and only then, I felt something welling up within me. I stood up and expounded the Bible for some 10 minutes — much to the dismay of the group. It turned out that not only did they believe that everyone who was 'baptised in the Spirit' spoke in tongues; they also believed it was wrong for women to teach. They avoided us for the rest of the evening.

It wasn't long before teaching became a major issue for me. I was continuing to read my Bible, and now it seemed fresh and life-giving. Working my way through the New Testament, I came to Romans 12:1-8, with its exhortation that Christians dedicate themselves wholeheartedly to exercising the spiritual gifts they are given. It was already clear that I had a gift for teaching the Bible. But then I came across 1 Corinthians 14:33 b-35:

'As in all the churches of the saints, the women should keep silence

in the churches. For they are not permitted to speak, but should be subordinate, as even the law says ... it is shameful for a woman to speak in church.'

Those verses were a body blow. How was I to reconcile Paul's injunction in Romans to use the gift of teaching I had been given, with his ban in Corinthians on women speaking in church? An old dilemma was reawakened. Since my vision of Jesus and the apostles as a young child, I had felt I was called to follow in my father's footsteps as a minister. But women couldn't be ministers. And, oddly, I was more inclined to think God had made a mistake in making me a girl, than in calling me to ministry.

Now I really needed to sort this matter out. I started by applying three evangelical principles: the Bible, in its original manuscripts, is without error; the Bible does not contradict itself; one scripture can be used to interpret another. Clearly I was going to need to know the Bible very well in order to solve the seeming contradiction. For the next twelve years I followed the M'Cheyne Bible reading calendar, which took me through the Old Testament annually and the New Testament twice a year; I used commentaries and other study aids; and I varied the Bible translations I read.

Meanwhile my parents and I had returned to England, where my father became pastor of an Evangelical Free church, and I had begun a degree in English Literature at Sussex University. I chose Sussex because it was our nearest university and they were willing to take me at very short notice. We didn't know that Sussex, then new, had a name for being radical. One feature of the English degree was that literary texts were studied within the historical, political, and social context in which they were written. Since all my schooling had taken place in the USA I had a lot to learn. I was surprised to find that the Puritans, so revered in the USA, were regarded with suspicion among the English literati.

Faiths Lost and Found

Rodney Hillman, who taught poetry and the English novel, was a sensitive and kind man who took a real interest in his students. He was influenced, as I recall, by William Empson's *7 Types Of Ambiguity* and F. R. Leavis on the intertwining of moral interest and form in literature. I learned the functions of creative tension, symbolism, imagery, and metaphor in poetry and fiction; an understanding which worked into my hitherto fairly literalist reading of the Bible. It was all challenging for a conservative evangelical. I think my tutors found me challenging, too. My personal tutor described me as 'rather astringent', which was clearly a polite way of putting it.

Still, I enjoyed my time at Sussex. A lecture on the Bloomsbury Set by the aged Quentin Bell was memorable, as was a two-term interdisciplinary seminar on the Industrial Revolution with Profs Laurence Lerner (who had taught Seamus Heaney) and Barry Supple. I studied Plato, Virgil, and Dante (in translation) with Stephen Medcalf, an eccentric high Anglican with a formidable intellect. Medcalf resembled a more rotund version of the young Beethoven; the drifts of books and papers in his office grew ever deeper, while the splash of egg yolk on his waistcoat never changed over the three years I was there. His teaching on Virgil's *Aeneid* had its own impact on me. Aeneas, arriving in Carthage, is prepared for conflict until he sees that the Carthaginians, like him, see 'tears in the nature of things' ['*sunt lacrimae rerum*']. Used to evangelical triumphalism, I'd never thought of the recognition of human suffering as a unifying force.

I made a number of friends who didn't share my Christian faith – including Persian Muslims and English atheists – and explored Brighton's rich cultural offerings. My horizons were being broadened. Some of the quotations recorded in the notebook I kept at the time show how my thinking was beginning to change:

46

'It must be admitted — and I have noticed it before — that nothing exceeds the licence occasionally taken by the imagination of very rigid people.' Henry James, *The Europeans*

'I well know by experience how [Calvinism] straitens the heart, and like rust corrodes the vitals of charity, having been myself tied and bound with Calvin's galling chain in times past.' Thomas Hartley in *Paradise Restored* (1764). (I owe this quote to historian Peter Lineham, who was researching his PhD in Swedenborgianism at Sussex while I was there.)

'To understand, thoroughly understand her own heart, was the first endeavour.' Jane Austen, *Emma.*

In Brighton I attended an Evangelical Free Church which was even more Calvinist than my father's. Both were members of the tiny Countess of Huntingdon's Connexion. One Sunday morning I decided to try an Anglican church which was said to be lively and popular with students. I must have chosen the wrong service, because I was the only young person there. I was handed two shabby books on entry and then ignored. We were never told what book to use or page number to turn to. I was completely lost, and when the service ended I departed, vowing never to try the Church of England again.

My father's pastorate was not going well, and my parents decided to return to the USA. They left in September 1976, a couple of weeks before my first final exam (at Sussex the finals were spaced throughout the last year). Dad and Mum repeatedly pressed me to return to the States to live with them after graduation. Their tactics were increasingly manipulative and the pressure intense. I was beginning to realise how controlling they were, and I had a sense that If I didn't make a break now I never would. It was going to be difficult to make my own way in what was essentially a strange country, but I was determined.

After graduation I moved to Eastbourne to take up a job as editorial assistant for Kingsway, an evangelical Christian publishing company. There my two closest colleagues, Charles Henshall and Richard Herkes, were evangelical Anglicans and really quite human. Richard and his wife Jenny became friends. I got new insights into the Church of England. Meanwhile I stayed with the familiar, and joined an Evangelical Free CoHC church which I will call Ichabod Chapel. I hadn't been there very long when the pastor had a breakdown and left, and the deacons decided not to call another pastor. They wanted to move the church towards the Restorationist (also called 'Shepherding') movement, which aimed to restore the Church to its first-century purity and unity.

Our last three years in the States had been spent in California, where the Jesus Movement was at its height. In Sussex I had no car, so little chance to explore the charismatic scene. Friends had taken me to a renewal meeting at Capel in Surrey, which was led by two young men called Clive Calver and Graham Kendrick. The group was small and there was not much freedom in the atmosphere. I felt sorry for the two leaders.

Now, with Ichabod Chapel's growing involvement in the Restorationist movement, I was back on the charismatic scene. It was very different, however, from the largely spontaneous Jesus Movement I had left behind in California a few years previously. Restorationism was authoritarian and highly structured. Its leaders were called 'apostles', and 'shepherds' were appointed under them. Everyone was supposed to be 'in submission' to (or, in the movement's language, 'covered by') a male leader. Women were not allowed to teach or to lead.

This was difficult, since after years of study I was now satisfied that it was not unbiblical for women to minister. Others at Ichabod were uneasy about developments, and I didn't like the arrogance with which the concerns of even long-established members were dismissed. The atmosphere in the church grew increasingly tense and some left.

For three months I got up and dressed for church every Sunday morning, but couldn't bring myself to go. I was longing for more thoughtful worship. The first book I had read after being baptised in the Spirit back in 1971 had been the selected letters of St Bernard of Clairvaux. I had been impressed by St Bernard's luminous wisdom, and that came to seem significant.

Finally I decided I had to try somewhere different. On Easter Sunday morning 1980 I went to All Saints, a nearby Anglican church. That same afternoon my 'shepherd' and his wife from Ichabod turned up unannounced and harangued me for hours in front of my flatmates and a dinner guest. 'If you leave Ichabod,' they said, 'you'll never be able to commit to another church again.' I returned to All Saints that evening.

Having been made redundant by Kingsway, I was now working in a Christian bookshop. That gave me a nodding acquaintance with most of the local clergy and active laypeople. I noticed that the Anglican women seemed to have more confidence than those from Ichabod, and assumed this was due to their being treated as equals in their churches. I wasn't to know that it was probably public-school polish.

I explored the possibility of joining the Church of England. To me the obvious place to begin was by reading the *Preface to the Book of Common Prayer* and the *Thirty-nine Articles*. To someone reared on the Reformation they seemed reassuringly familiar. I discussed my questions and concerns with the vicar of All Saints, Gordon Rideout. Gordon, a conservative evangelical from the Reformed wing of the Church, gave me some leaflets by the Victorian evangelical bishop J. C. Ryle. Convinced that the

Church of England was 'sound', I decided to join. When I told my former Kingsway colleague Richard, he replied, 'Oh good, now you can be a deaconess.' It was not until a year later, on the eve of my confirmation, that I plucked up the courage to tell my parents I'd become an Anglican. I got no reply; it was my sisters who told me our parents had disowned me.

I went through selection and training for the Anglican ministry. The selectors seemed surprised when I traced my move towards Anglicanism back to studying symbolism in literature. They recommended I be a university chaplain. My fellow ordinands were astonished to hear that reading the *Preface* and *Thirty-nine Articles* had been the final clincher – few of them had read and even fewer valued those foundational documents. I was ordained deacon in 1987, and very soon learned that the Church did not in fact treat women as equals. Ordination to the priesthood followed in 1994. The battle over women's ordination was often bitter, and many of us who were pioneers still carry our scars.

I served a curacy in a charismatic church, St Hilarius ('St Hi'), which advocated John Wimber's 'power healing' and 'power evangelism'. I hadn't before encountered Wimber but was soon trained in his methods and, along with other church staff, attended several of his conferences. At two of them I had profound spiritual experiences which I still believe to have been genuine. I became increasingly concerned about his methods, however, and about how I saw them being taught and used. Two friends who were doctors observed that the Wimber healing technique relied on the power of suggestion – in other words, it was hypnosis. I began to notice that people who had been 'healed' often relapsed a few weeks or months later. Those who had serious conditions that didn't respond to the Wimber method were usually ignored or neglected. I took on the visiting of some of these chronically ill people. Naturally, these invalids were also questioning St Hi's commitment to the Wimber technique.

My unease increased when John Wimber associated himself with the Kansas City Prophets and Paul Cain. These 'prophets' claimed to be restoring the biblical gift of prophecy to the Church, and that Britain would undergo a spiritual revival beginning in October 1990. That revival didn't happen. My concerns were more fundamental, however. In the Bible prophets usually proclaim the word and the will of God, and call people back to his ways of justice and true worship. The Kansas City Prophets were doing some of that, but much of their ministry consisted in making personal predictions about individuals. This impinged on me directly when Paul Cain interested himself in our church – or at least, in my two male clergy colleagues. This enabled me to see how the technique worked. A prediction was made about a church leader already known to Wimber; in our case, the vicar. The prophecy seemed apt but was decidedly vague, so Cain was contacted for more information. In the course of an hour's conversation he elicited a good deal of information about the church, which enabled him to make further credible-sounding prophecies. It's a process called 'cold reading' which is often employed by psychics and fortune tellers. I watched Cain and others of the 'prophets' employing this technique at two Wimber conferences in October 1990. At one, Cain singled out Chris Brain, then leader of Sheffield's Nine O'Clock Service, by name and prophesied about God's blessing. Five years later Brain was found to have been sexually abusing a number of women in his congregation, including at the time of Cain's prophecy. The Holy Spirit didn't see fit to tell Cain of this.

The Holy Spirit also neglected to inform Cain that there were three ordained people at St Hi's, not just two. When Cain gave a public prophecy for the church mentioning only the two male clergy, the vicar's response was to tell me, 'If God doesn't want you here, maybe you shouldn't be an elder, either.'

During the last year of my curacy I was increasingly sidelined. Those who were enthusiastic about the Kansas City Prophets and Wimber were getting the message that I was not 'moving with the Spirit'. Some of those I had been closest to ostracised me, and social invitations from some quarters stopped. On one occasion I was being prayed for before a service, as was usual, and didn't respond in the way that was expected. The group began to pray I would be delivered from evil spirits. Once again I was considered to be disobeying God, and it hurt.

Looking back, I can see that it was difficult for the vicar to have a curate who was not only not 'moving with the Spirit' (or at least, in the direction the vicar wanted for the church), but was also asking challenging questions. At the same time, I was there to be trained, and asking questions is an important way to explore and learn. Ever since, I have advised people never to join a group (or follow a leader) that isn't comfortable with their asking questions.

During that last year I was invited to join a small group of experts in different fields – neurology, medicine, religious history, music – who were exploring the overlap between psychology, spirituality, emotion, and physiology. All of them were sceptical about Wimber's techniques, and those of others who claimed to practise healing and deliverance. Those meetings proved significant for me at least, proving foundational for a research degree I later completed, and much of the work I have done since.

I was fortunate to have also a spiritual director who was able to help with my questions. Sr Marion Eva OHP pointed me to some of the classic writing on spiritual experience. I found St Teresa of Avila's book *The Interior Castle* a great help. Teresa was very familiar with mystical and what we might call charismatic experiences, but counselled that it was a mistake to focus on them. Such experiences, which she called 'consolations', had little significance in themselves; our focus should remain on Jesus. As I looked at what was going on around me I could see the wisdom of this. Some of the St Hi's congregation relied on phenomena such as people being 'slain in the spirit' (falling over) or being overcome with emotion as signs that God was there. The corollary was that if such spectacles were absent, they doubted God's presence. And it took increasingly extreme phenomena to produce the same spiritual 'high': they were addicted to charismatic experience. Equally, some lived faithful Christian lives but doubted their faith because they had never experienced any visions or visitations. I remain very grateful for my own charismatic experiences, but cautious about a number of features of the charismatic movement.

As the years went on I also became uncomfortable with the attitudes of some of the more closed conservative evangelicals. When I was ordained to the priesthood a Roman Catholic neighbour gave me a silver crucifix which had been blessed by the then Pope. It meant a great deal to her and I was touched. A Free Church conservative evangelical once challenged me for wearing it, saying, 'Our Lord came down from the cross!' 'Yes, but it's good to be reminded that he was once on the cross,' I replied. This wasn't enough for my challenger, who wouldn't let the matter drop even after I explained why the crucifix was significant for me.

On another occasion I was sitting next to an Anglican conservative evangelical (I'll call him Steve) during a lecture on Galatians. Afterwards Steve complained that the lecturer 'keeps saying Galatians is about grace, when it's clearly about the law'. Since the consensus of commentators is that Galatians does indeed prize grace above Old Testament law, I queried his statement. His reply: 'We have to have law, so that we know who's in and who's out.' That attitude seems to me to contradict the gospel, which is about including those who were previously 'out' under the Law. Moreover, in his parable of the wheat and the tares Jesus implied that it's very difficult to know who is 'in' and who 'out', until the final judgment. (The truth of this has since been proved when conservative evangelical leaders Jonathan Fletcher, John Smyth, and my old mentor Gordon Rideout were found to have been guilty of abuse.)

Later I stood for General Synod. At the hustings Steve asked what my stance on homosexuality was. I replied, truthfully, that I was currently studying the Scriptures on the topic and had not yet arrived at a conclusion. A couple of weeks later I was told that Steve had been ringing members of the diocesan evangelical fellowship to tell them I was not orthodox, and they shouldn't vote for me. I was shocked. Not only was this a dirty campaigning tactic, but I hadn't before encountered the view that a person's attitude towards homosexuality was a test of orthodoxy. Moreover, I had been brought up to emulate the Bereans, who 'were more noble than those in Thessalonica, in that they received the word with all readiness of mind, and searched the scriptures daily, whether those things were so' (Acts 17:11 KJV). How could an evangelical condemn another evangelical out of hand for searching the scriptures on a controversial topic? When did toeing the party line become more important than continuing to explore and learn from the Bible?

We human beings have a deep need to relate and to belong; we are created in the image of a God who is three persons in perfect harmony. But our sense of belonging should never depend on excluding others, defining them as 'not belonging'. The Jesus I see in the gospels and Acts is always encouraging us to look outwards, to open our minds and hearts to those we instinctively fear or despise. I came to see that I hung on to some aspects of evangelical identity long after I should have let them go, because I was unwilling to lose that security. I don't need to do that now, because my security is in the matchless love of God.

I intend to keep exploring. I have found these words, from C. S. Lewis's novel *Prince Caspian*, to be true:

'Aslan,' said Lucy, 'you're bigger.'

'That is because you are older, little one,' answered he.

'Not because you are?'

'I am not. But every year you grow, you will find me bigger.'

Dorset, Knightsbridge and Byzantium

Charles Foster

I had the privilege of an English boarding school education.

That meant I was emotionally stunted, cunning, manipulative, almost incapable of honest relationships, superficially confident and profoundly insecure. Such security as I had came from the certainties encoded in the hierarchies of clan and society. I was told I was at the top of the social tree, and saw no reason to doubt it. Self-examination was psychologically impossible: if I had seen what was really in there I'd have broken up – as some sensitives did. Introspection was, in any event, effete. It would have been deadly to express any emotion other than enthusiasm for the house or school on the river or the cricket pitch, or visceral distaste for the lower orders. It just wasn't *done* – even if one did have any emotions to express. Certainly *love* didn't have anything to do with what you did with the girls bussed in for the house dance.

I was, in other words, a perfect candidate for the conservative evangelical Iwerne movement which tracked me down as soon as I arrived at university. I've written elsewhere about this movement and my place in it, and I'm not going to repeat (most of) it here. It's enough to say that they didn't want to *change* anything at all about me, other than to add theological certainty to my list of self-defining attributes. They didn't want me to grow in any way: quite the opposite. They wanted to crystallise and theologise everything that boarding school had done: to sanctify the stuntedness and to make a virtue of the self-evasion, the distrust of emotion and the disdain for relationship. Iwerne was, they assured me, the ultimately prestigious club. It was all male, all white, all public school (and not just any old public school, old chap; just the top few), and once in, you were in it for life and, thereafter, for eternity (where, don't worry, you won't have to mix with the hoi polloi). Until you went to the leafier suburbs of heaven (commuting to the centre each day, of course, for God would want to bend your ear when dealing with a particularly knotty problem), St Helen's Bishopsgate or Emmanuel, Wimbledon would look after you, keep you from loose women and troubling questions, and cook you meat and two veg on Sundays until you had married (no hand-holding first, mind you) one of the fragrant 'lady helpers' from the Iwerne constituency.

The mission was, very explicitly, to convert the 'top' people, on the understanding (a theological version of trickle-down economics) that if you converted them, the rest of the world, being constitutionally followers of the officer class, would come meekly into line. And who were the 'top' people – the people who God particularly wanted; the anointed ones? They were people like me, because I was a top chap myself. I'd never have to rub shoulders with anyone who hadn't been expensively educated. I'd never have to learn a different social language. It was all very satisfactory.

What a club. Who wouldn't want to join? And the entry fee? All I had to do was to mumble my agreement to the doctrine of penal substitution, turn up each week to a prayer meeting and to the annual summer camps in Dorset for schoolboys from *the* schools, exude a hearty tweediness, and not be found reading the Egyptian Book of the Dead or sleeping with the girlfriend I wasn't supposed to have anyway.

I signed up without hesitation. I didn't believe the theology, of course – or I knew that there was a lot more to say than that. But boarding school makes you a supreme compartmentaliser. It was essential for survival. You might be a fiery anarchist in one section of your wizened soul, and a bowler-hatted banker in another. The anarchist and the banker wouldn't trouble one another. Integration was for poofs and poets. We were men of the world and, if it pleased us, the otherworld too.

And so I preached and postured and prayed for years, moonlighting blithely as a communist, a lothario, a Buddhist and an entranced child. The various lives gave piquancy to one another. It was great. I could have it all. The only problem was that there was no 'I' there at all to enjoy it.

But the 'I' will out. And it came out, terrifyingly, when I was on a very long and very lonely expedition in the Sinai desert. It bellowed. It said that it couldn't take any more of this; that it would die very soon if I didn't do something radical.

The details of what happened next don't matter for these purposes. But right after that expedition, with the sand still in my socks, I found myself standing in Holy Trinity Brompton (HTB) – the church famous for the Alpha Course – with tears gushing down my face and a sensation of being physically filled, from my toes to the top of my head, with something that was Good, and which revived the 'I' sufficiently for the I to say, and mean it: '*I* believe'. The walls of those compartments stood no chance: the Good dissolved them all.

'How are you?', asked a friend who saw me shortly afterwards.

'I can breathe', I replied. 'And since I've not been able to do that before, it'll be interesting to see what happens next.'

It doesn't sound like much of a revolution. A journey from one posh London church run by public schoolboys to yet another. But it was.

I stayed at HTB for years. It taught me much of what I know about the great adventure of being a human. I'd been taught that the Holy Spirit was mainly important as an aid to Bible study – a sort of ghostly Scripture Union notes. HTB taught me that there was rather more to the Holy Spirit than that. It taught me that real men cried, sometimes changed nappies, and that real women sometimes preached and sometimes guiltlessly watched the nappy-changing; that relationship was everything, that it wasn't heretical to care about social justice, that the church included Catholics and Orthodox and many others besides, that humans are embodied beings and that therefore pouring tea wasn't necessarily a time-wasting distraction from the real business of evangelism, and raising hands in worship wasn't necessarily hysteria warranting medical intervention. It taught me that God loved far more than he fulminated; that he could heal even retrospectively – reaching far back into the Darwinian dormitories of my teens; that humans were created equal and adored passionately; that unless there's something very wrong with us we bleed into one another; that debates about the mechanics of salvation risked draining salvation of its wonder; that the Sermon on the Mount and the Magnificat meant what they said, and that the meek really would inherit the earth and the mighty would be put down from their seat, and that heaven probably wasn't a black tie event. It taught me the imperative of gratitude, the centrality of joy, and the legitimacy of ecstasy. It taught me that mountains are highly mobile, and that the devil hates good music and poetry. It taught me that without self-examination you didn't really know of what you should repent, but that you should try to be kind to yourself, because God would be, and you should try to emulate him. It taught me that stuff is complicated, and that complexity isn't necessarily demonic. It taught me that reality isn't algorithmic, and so theology shouldn't be either. It taught me that though we may be fallen, it was possible to fall only because we are really, truly, actually made in the image of God. It taught me that humans are of infinite weight. It taught me that God (as C. S. Lewis observed) is the great iconoclast, continually smashing up the mere ideas we have about him, and that we should expect to leave church each Sunday changed. It taught me that mere assent to a catechismal proposition means in itself nothing whatever, and that if you think that it determines your eternal destiny you know nothing about either the subconscious or New Testament Greek. It taught me grace, where I had known only law. It didn't snigger at and denigrate romantic love. It taught me the meaning of sacrament, taught me that everything humans do is sacramental, and schooled me in the liturgy necessary to make each sacrament good rather than bad. It also gave me some amazing feeds, many vats of red wine, and a host of brilliant, enduring, irreverent friends who mocked me with merciless kindness until some of my pomposity shrank just a little.

Some might be surprised that a move from Iwerne/St Helen's to HTB might be seen as a defection. Aren't they both evangelical, and both pretty conservative?

HTB eschews the label 'evangelical'. That's wise, though widely misunderstood. 'Evangelical' carries too much baggage, and if you adopt the name you'll find yourself lumped in with some intolerable company. HTB prefers to say that it is 'Christian'. To say that you believe in 'Mere Christianity' is a big claim, and might sound presumptuous. I'm not going to suggest what the lowest common denominators of 'Christianity' are, or whether

HTB is 'merely Christian'. But I'm entirely confident in saying that whatever goes on at HTB is at least part of – and the essential core of – historic Christianity. I hadn't met historic Christianity until I stood there tearfully in my sandy socks.

For the Iwerne contingent, anyway, HTB was well beyond the Pale. The Iwerne Pale, that is, perceived as coextensive with the Kingdom of Heaven. A move to HTB was highly offensive: a betrayal far more fundamental than Kim Philby's. Not only was I sitting in Red Square, Knightsbridge, clutching and no doubt sharing a folder full of those deliciously arcane secrets of the Iwerne Officers' Room, but (and this made it worse than Philby – who at least had the good manners to have a wretched time in Russia) I was apparently having a ball, and couldn't stop telling everyone that I was.

At Iwerne and throughout the Iwerne archipelago, it's impossible to distinguish between theology and culture. This is a consequence of a perverted kind of Calvinism. The thinking goes something like this: We're elected to our position in life (socially elevated) and in eternity (predestined for glory). Since the source of both types of election is the same (God) the two types of election are the same. Our self-applauding chauvinism is thus sanctified. To question it is sacrilege; to defend it is a holy obligation. 'Iwerne is my church', Jonathan Fletcher, the disgraced High Priest of Iwerne is quoted as saying – so donating to some summer camps for public schoolboys the authority of the apostles and prescribing the duty of martyrdom for those camps and their culture.

This, I think, explains the particular offence to Iwernites of HTB. For the HTB hierarchy in my day (it's changed since) should (it was thought by Iwerne) have been Iwerne chaps themselves. The vicar, Sandy Millar, and the two curates, Nicky Gumbel and Nicky Lee had all gone to Eton and Trinity College, Cambridge.

They were prime candidates for club membership. Yet they hadn't even applied. That was deeply offensive: an offence against the club, and so against God and his anointed club members. It was also rather troubling, if you let yourself think about it, for why would anyone eligible not want to join? Added to all that were the intolerable facts that HTB had a vast international ministry and seemed supremely happy.

I've hinted above at some of the theological differences between Iwerne and HTB. Some are differences of emphasis. Some are not. Iwerne, if pressed, would insist that HTB sets experience above The Word (always capitalised in speech, and by which Iwerne really means R. A. Torrey's *What the Bible Teaches*, Debrett's, and possibly Wisden). In any event, add together a number of differences of emphasis and you soon have a difference of substance. To me, then and now, the differences seemed and seem theologically and personally vast. And I know that they seemed and seem vast too to the Iwerne establishment.

So how was the news from Red Square received? What did Iwerne do and say?

Nothing: absolutely nothing.

I wasn't a significant figure in the Iwerne establishment. I was a junior 'officer' (we loved those military titles) with no access to the inner circle. I wasn't sufficiently sporty or good-looking, and hadn't become a clergyman or a schoolmaster in one of the strategic schools. But I'd shinned some way up the greasy pole. I gave talks at the Iwerne camps themselves, and at the Iwerne schools. I'd kept the Book of the Dead well hidden. My defection meant *something*.

But nothing happened. It wasn't as if I severed contact with the Iwerne lot. I tried hard to see them, and for a while, on my initiative, I saw several of them quite often. They knew very well that I'd crossed the border. I enthused to them about HTB. The topic was abruptly shut down. And when I stopped issuing the invitations, the meetings stopped completely.

I didn't exist. I hadn't ever existed. I was airbrushed out of the photos of those beaming men and boys romping spiritually through the perpetual Dorset sunshine.

Why didn't they remonstrate with me? Seek to convince me of the error of my ways? Try to fish me out of the lake of fire? Remind me fraternally of the Parable of the Prodigal Son and tell me the dates of the next camps? Because, I think, to remonstrate would be to admit that the defection had happened, and that would mean admitting that the club had been found wanting. They couldn't say: 'Foster's been led away by the devil' — *for the elect are predestined to salvation.* What, then, were their options? There were only two, given their view of election. They could admit that the club had been wrong, and had misidentified me as one of the elect. But the club was divine and infallible! How could it make a mistake so fundamental? Or they could pretend the defection had never happened, and that the old certainties were still in place. That's what they did.

Iwerne's response to malefactors far more important than I ever was suggests that this analysis is right. The scandals of John Smyth and Jonathan Fletcher should have shaken the whole Iwerne-based conservative evangelical movement to the core. They haven't. Yes, the PR people told Iwerne that it had to express remorse, and apologise, and there was some shrewdly choreographed hand-wringing. Inquiries into the culture that facilitated the abuse were launched, and we were assured that lessons have been learned. The Iwerne camps themselves were formally dissolved — the name Iwerne was just too toxic. But the dissolution was really a rebranding.

I'm sounding more cynical than I am. I don't doubt the

sincerity of those who apologised. I don't doubt, either, that many individuals who loved Iwerne and knew and trusted Smyth and Fletcher were personally hurt and confused. But the movement itself sees Smyth and Fletcher as bad apples in an essentially wholesome barrel. And everyone makes mistakes sometimes, don't they? No need to get overexcited.

The camps today are not those I knew: they are less overtly hierarchical and less buttoned-up. There are women there (and not just in the kitchens) which means that there's a lot more emotional intelligence sloshing around. There is indeed less to reform than there was in the bad old days. Yet still, despite Smyth and Fletcher, the mission, the theology, and the fatal conflation of theology and culture remain the same. Despite the movement's fulsome acknowledgement of some failings in ethos and governance, there has been no systematic interrogation of the theological justifications that provided both the background of the abuse and the failure over many years to deal with it. It's assumed that the theology is sound, but that it was wielded ham-fistedly and in some instances pervertedly. To question the theology is unthinkable. And so it has not been thought.

Too many whistles were blown, and it wasn't possible, eventually, for the Iwerne movement to pretend that Smyth and Fletcher had never existed, or that they hadn't really gone astray. Had that been feasible I suspect it would have happened. It would have been dealt with in-house – on the genuinely-believed understanding that the Kingdom would be damaged more if things became public. John Smyth, after all, was allowed to creep off to Africa, where his collar could not easily be fingered by the English police. It was the nearest possible thing to a denial (to the movement as well as to the world) that anything untoward had ever occurred. Look at the massive delays in the emergence of the Smyth and Fletcher stories.

Of course there's a world of difference between my defection and the fall of Smyth and Fletcher. I moved camps: they didn't. They remained (in Smyth's case), and remain (in Fletcher's) wholly committed to the theology and ethos of Iwerne. But there's an enlightening parallel too. If something's unthinkable, don't think it.

I didn't stay at HTB, though I gratefully acknowledge my debt. Having moved from Dorset to Bishopsgate to Sinai to Knightsbridge, I finally found my way, via Jerusalem, to Constantinople, and was received into the Greek Orthodox Church. It's a long story. I am in the home I had been seeking at least since birth, and very possibly before.

The move to Eastern Orthodoxy generates a coda to the Iwerne story. For after my reception (a comforting word) the Iwernites came out of the woodwork. They were happy to talk to me about Orthodoxy as they were not happy to talk about HTB.

Why might that be? It may simply be that we were all older and less insecure by then. But I don't think so. I think it is because they saw the shift to Orthodoxy as reassuring evidence that I was mad – and had been mad all along. Orthodoxy had nothing to do with their Christianity – and therefore with Christianity itself. Orthodoxy had a strong apophatic inflection, for instance. It tended to the view that one could make only negative assertions about God. How ridiculous! God was entirely knowable: in fact the essential truths about him could be encapsulated in a 15 minute, three point talk to teenagers. Orthodoxy could be discussed as a matter of exotic anthropology, as HTB could not. Those heavily bearded Athonites couldn't row or play cricket, and would never have been invited to the club, and if I had thrown in my lot with them, that explained the constitutional derangement of mind that had resulted in the HTB debacle all those years ago. If a certified madman left the club, one could be all the more confident that the club was the place to be.

I know that this chapter is supposed to be about Iwerne's view of my heresy. But of course there's another case study embedded here – my graceless view of *Iwerne's* heresy. It's worth saying that HTB would be appalled at my uncharity in describing conservative evangelicalism. But, as is obvious, I'm angry. Not so much at what the movement did to me. I got out early, and relatively unscathed. But at what it did to others. At the shrivelled lives. At the experiences frustrated, the books unread and the thoughts nipped in the bud. At the marriages that never were because they were deemed 'unhelpful'. Anyway, I've tried to keep in touch with some of my Iwerne friends. Many of them are superb people. I'd just like to see them fly, because they'd be astonishing. We talk about Orthodoxy if they want to. We tend to stay off Iwerne. There's no point.

I tell myself that I meet with them because I like them. But perhaps there's more to it than that. Perhaps I want to be told by the Iwerne top brass that I'm all right really. Perhaps I never really escaped after all.

But of self-psychoanalysis there is no end. That is fortunately not true of chapters.

Traditional Christianity to Queer Authenticity

Thomas Bohache

'Exodus' (literally, 'a coming out of') is a notion familiar to many, especially those who have been or felt oppressed or 'othered' in some way by society or one of its component groups. The biblical concept of the Exodus involves the Hebrews (later to become the Jews) leaving the bondage and oppression of slavery in Egypt for potential freedom and fulfilment in the Promised Land. Every year observant Jews commemorate this event at Passover. In addition, and perhaps more important in my formation, ever since the story was repeated, it has been claimed by new generations seeking an end to oppression, whether or not in a religious context. As part of the LGBTQ+ community(ies), I am one who has lived with exodus: Either I have decided intentionally to leave a church, or I have been made to feel that I should depart. Not just once, unfortunately, but several times, both with and without drama. My exodi have, for the most part, involved not church fights or formal excommunication, but rather my own grappling with the intersection of religion and personhood, which, for me, are always commingled.

I believe that religion, at its very best, calls us to wholeness and personal authenticity. Good theology, good ethics, and good ecclesiology should be engaged in the pursuit of authentic personhood for all of God's creatures. For some this seems relatively easy or is largely unquestioned; for others it is extremely difficult, as it was (and is) for me. Oftentimes, this is a process that never ends; it is in fact a journey, and, as several feminists remind us, 'the journey is our home.' Moreover, each journey is individual, even within a religious community. No one else has had or will have the exact same journey that I describe here. Social groups may have similar perspectives or lived experiences, but no two journeys are exactly the same. Indeed, no two exodi or 'comings out' (an important term for every LGBTQ person) are the same.

∾

Before I describe my journey, I should like to describe myself and my social location. Today, I am a white, middle-class, well-educated, pro-feminist gay man who sometimes identifies as queer. I am a retired pastor, educator, and writer, closer now to seventy than sixty, currently living with a disability acquired as a result of COVID-19 delta pneumonia. I have been happily married to my husband for seventeen years. We have been together for twenty. I was born and raised in the United States, in a devout Roman Catholic family. The three most important components of my personhood, in the order in which I embraced them, are Catholicism, gayness, and feminism.

I am from Los Angeles (LA), California, already a large metropolitan area when I was born in 1955, and a huge one now. The L.A. metro area is made up of lots of towns or small cities that were not quite suburbs because all of it was referred to as 'L.A.,' and many folks did not ever go 'downtown,' a place I've seen only a handful of times. In addition, there were unincorporated areas of Los Angeles County, such as where we lived, that had a Los Angeles address but were not within the city limits.

We were a rather traditional, staunch Roman Catholic family: We attended Mass every Sunday and on all holy days; We fasted and abstained as required during Lent; during my early childhood we had meatless Fridays, until changes from the Second Vatican Council relaxed the restriction. We were quite active in our parish, which was geographically established within the Archdiocese of Los Angeles, the regional governmental unit of the Roman Catholic Church. My sisters and I attended Catholic schools from kindergarten through high school. Grade school was co-educational and administered by the parish, with principal and faculty who were mostly nuns with a few laywomen; the high schools we chose were segregated by gender and composed of students from all parishes in the Archdiocese. Girls' high schools had all women teachers, mostly nuns, when my sisters attended; my high school was staffed by Jesuit priests, seminarians, and laymen, with two laywomen added to the faculty during my senior year.

When I was growing up, Los Angeles was not nearly as diverse, and what diversity there was appeared to be grouped together. Then, as now, there were areas that were more Latin or black, some that included predominantly those of European descent, and some that were more integrated, usually dependent upon income; thus, the parish demographics were affected by its geographical location. Our parish before my tenth birthday was mostly white, with very few Mexican Americans or African Americans; more diversity occurred as I grew older, facilitated and hindered by 'white flight'. By the time I graduated from grade school, my class had quite a few non-whites, but no one spoke with an accent or was other than middle to upper middle class. High school, being composed of many different parish members, was more heterogeneous. Many races, ethnicities, and economic levels were represented, and some received scholarships. I did not meet a Jew until I was in high school, and I did not meet a Muslim or Hindu until I was in college at the University of California, Los Angeles (UCLA). The only 'ethnic' restaurants we knew were Americanised versions of Italian, Mexican, and Chinese.

I describe all of this to emphasise that my earliest years were lived within a monoculture largely determined by the parish within which my family's location and income placed me; moreover, this monoculture was both heteropatriarchal and heteronormative. The burgeoning feminist movement had not reached our parish by the time I left it, and I only heard stirrings of it at UCLA. The Stonewall Riots that launched the gay liberation movement occurred in New York the year I entered high school, but I did not know about it until years later. Homosexuality was not openly discussed, and the only 'transexual' was entertainer Christine Jorgenson, who wrote what was considered a lurid book about her sex change, which in turn became a titillating movie. 'Normal' (i.e., heterosexual) people went 'slumming,' as it were, by attending drag shows in disreputable parts of town. My family was pretty much like the ones depicted on *Leave It to Beaver* and *Father Knows Best*. I lived through what my husband and I call 'the tyranny of the heterosexual family' and what in other writings I have termed 'heterocolonialism' – the construction and maintenance of a heterosexually-based society from the top down. Both of these concepts exist today, their maintenance often determined by political ebbs and flows.

What I knew of the Civil Rights Movement growing up was largely filtered through dinner table conversation. Today I understand that my parents and our fellow white parishioners were racist, but in those days people in California reserved that term for overt racists from the Deep South whom they heard about and saw on the evening news or in films. The conversations I heard about race as a boy were concerns that there were more blacks moving into the parish and the difference between these 'militant n*****s' and the 'nice colored people' who already lived there (i.e., those who spoke and acted like white people). Mexican Americans (without accents) were considered Caucasians and therefore white. Chinese and Japanese were of another race but were 'model minorities' and smarter than everybody else. There were no southeast Asians or those from the Indian sub-continent in the parish.

My father was the absolute head of the family, and, although I didn't see him all that much until high school, he was clearly the rulemaker and chief enforcer. My mother was a housewife, later a 'homemaker', and now would be called a 'stay-at-home mom' (which I'm sure she would have loathed). My parents were very good providers, and I do not seek to cast aspersions on my family; but it was clear to me that my father's authority came from God as mediated through the Catholic Church. We were told what books we could not read and what movies we could not see, based on what the Church said through *The Tidings*, our diocesan newspaper, and reinforced every day by the nuns who, for the most part, were very young, sheltered, naïve, and indoctrinated women, fresh out of a Catholic liberal arts college.

I learned some very odd things from these nuns, by the way: that we would not have to go the bathroom if Adam and Eve hadn't eaten the apple; that syphilis (which someone asked about because Henry VIII died of it) was a disease one gets from 'touching dirty women'; and that Jesus hung on the crucifix in our classroom because we 'did that' since we were 'such bad children'. I also learned that boys were very different from girls, but not how. One nun gave the boys detention and extra homework for no apparent reason other than our gender. Despite all of this, however, I did emerge from Catholic school with a very good education, especially in the areas of reading, grammar, and spelling. My parents didn't want to hear anything potentially negative about priests and nuns. My father was from an old Czech Catholic family which had taught him, as he taught me, that priests and nuns spoke and acted for God. My mother, a convert from a little-practised Methodism, followed my father.

To summarise, my earliest feelings about how religion and personhood might be interrelated were those of unquestioning respect for authority and amorphous fear, under an Almighty Father God who resided over a Holy Mother Church, which dictated to 'the faithful' offspring below. Our household of authoritative father with non-equal mother over dependent children and more dependent pets mirrored what I experienced at church and school, where it was read from (edited) scriptures, preached from the pulpit, and taught in each class in some way – whether it be religion, English, bible history, geography, world history, or physical education. Feminist philosopher Mary Daly, herself a refugee from Catholicism, has summarised this hierarchical situation very well: 'When God is male, then the male is God.' But I didn't encounter this quote until I was in my thirties. As a young man all I knew was to accept it or suffer some unexplained consequences. In my adult journey I have learned that this sort of heteropatriarchal, usually but not always white, hierarchy is used to keep others 'in their place', that is, disenfranchised and marginalised and therefore oppressed. This system of interlocking oppression was starting to come to a head in the 1960s and 1970s, which is precisely when I was entering puberty and becoming aware of my sexual personhood. The dilemma I faced as someone who felt left out and othered at home, church, and school is what precipitated my exodus from Catholicism.

∽

My immediate family was made up of my parents, my two sisters, and me. I was the youngest, and by the time I first remember, the eldest was in high school and already dating and working during the summers as a nanny, after which she married while in college; thus, for a period of about ten years I was closer to my other sister, who was six years older, until she got married. As I have mentioned my father was not around much in those early years; in an effort to get me some (male?) socialisation, my mother took me to a nursery school where I could play with other boys. Alas, I did not want to do this; I didn't like the games they played, nor the endless discussion of war and guns, especially 'Cowboys and Indians'! I do remember hearing a discussion at a holiday gathering of extended family that my parents were afraid I was going to be a 'sissy'. I didn't know what that was, but the tone of the conversation made me realise that this was *not* the way to be. They mentioned two cousins who had been labelled a 'sissy' and a 'tomboy' but had turned out all right, since they were both married. This made me ask my mother later if I could be a 'tomboy' since I was called Tom, which made her laugh and exclaim that boys couldn't be tomboys. (I somehow knew not to ask her at this juncture what a sissy was).

The next year I was enrolled at the parish school for kindergarten. I would attend this school for the next nine years, with many of the same students for all those years, along with some additions and subtractions along the way. The kindergarten teacher was an older laywoman who had taught children from the same families for at least two generations. It was here in kindergarten that I learned what a sissy was – a gender traitor, a boy who acted like a girl. I liked playing jump rope and hopscotch with the girls. I despised being with the boys, whether it was playing ball or wrestling or pretending I was a soldier or a cowboy, especially if it involved a gun. The teacher announced to the class that 'if Tommy can't play with the rest of the boys, we'll have to put ribbons in his hair and paint his fingernails!' (Such a helpful woman; little did she know that this actually sounded quite appealing.) The same sentiment was repeated by the nuns I encountered in later grades, who called me a sissy in front of the class, causing all the other students to jeer at me, bump me in the cafeteria, and other physical and mental/emotional high jinks, so that school became one day after another of torture (what today would be acknowledged as bullying). I would try to tell my sister about this on our walks to and from school, but she didn't want to know about it because she was very popular and would often have her friends who lived in our neighborhood walk with us. She did tell me when I was in second grade and she in eighth that I needed to start getting along by myself because she was going to high school and wouldn't be there to protect me anymore. The solution for me was twofold: first, I determined to excel in academics, and second, I got particularly close to two nuns who would have me do special tasks and run errands for them. One of them became the principal, and she began having me organise the school supplies and do office work for her so that I could skip recess and lunch periods.

One thing that my special nuns couldn't do for me, however, was spare me from the dreaded 'P.E.' (physical education), which was segregated by gender. It was here the jeering and taunting became pretty bad, and I learned the words 'fairy', 'fag(got)', and 'queer', but didn't have any idea what these words meant, except that they indicated hatred and othering based on not being a 'real boy'. There were several of us boys who were no good at sports. We took turns being chosen last for teams and started associating with each other. When we wanted to sing in the choir, we were told by the nun who led the choir that we could not until we learned to play football! I watched the nuns encourage the crushes that developed between boys and girls beginning about fifth grade, and I wondered when I would feel that; I half-heartedly acted like I had a crush on the most popular girl because she and I were the best students in the class. Before too long, however, I realised that I had those feelings for one of the other outcast boys, who liked to talk about 'girlish' things, as did I, except he was not ashamed of it like I was. On the contrary, he was a rebel and did things to get himself in trouble, a trait I admired because I never wanted to rock any boats. If we had become closer friends I don't know if his positive view of himself would have rubbed off on me, but my mother put a halt to our friendship when she discovered he was black.

As I advanced through grade school, I was aware that more and more we were being reminded of the attributes that accrued to each gender (according to the mid-sixties mindset); and the more we learned this, the more it was stressed in the academic curriculum that this was a divine mandate. If we did not act in the way we were taught we were denying God, and God would deny us. The words 'homosexuality' and 'gay' were never mentioned, but somehow it became clear that gender traitors like me weren't desirable to the spirit God and His [sic] son, the (hu)man Jesus, whom we were studying and worshiping. This is where my parents' views of priests and nuns becomes important, because my sisters and I were taught that whatever these men and women said came from God Himself [sic]; thus, it was not only pointless to disagree or question anything but downright sinful. The result of this conditioning was that my oldest sister left the Church as soon as she married, my sister in the middle became extremely devout and has remained active and committed to the Church to this day, while I tried to stay and continued to wrestle with my personhood, only eventually to have an exodus with subsequent wandering in the desert.

High school did not help this very much. Not only was it an all-boy school, but the teachers were also male. There were men all around me, and my pubescent hormones were leading me to feel things for them that I was supposed to feel for girls. It was during the first two years of high school that I began to be aware that there were men who were known as homosexuals ('homos' for short), who lived life in contradiction to society's – and the Church's – dictates. They called themselves 'gay', but nobody else did. The priests began to tell us how horrible these men were, that they were going to hell, and that God hated them. They said if any of us were having those feelings we should tell them. They told us these men would try to make us 'do things', but no one ever explained what sex was or what two people of any gender did together. Our parents were supposed to tell us that. Mine, however, did not; I learned from forbidden books and conversations with others who experimented. I also learned that some of the priests were hypocrites and were not keeping their vows of chastity, and that a couple of boys who had gone to them with same sex feelings were either seduced instead or 'outed' to their parents. My own same sex attractions and anxiety accumulated until I was at an emotional breaking point, although outwardly no one seemed to notice. The problem was not just that I found myself gay in a straight world; more importantly, I was gay in a church whose representatives said I was going to hell and that God hated me. Since, according to all I'd been taught, the priests and nuns spoke for God, this was the message that summed up Christianity for me: that I was hated by God and had no remedy.

In high school I once again found other outcasts. This

time there were three of us. Each of us was grappling with our budding gay sexuality, but each of us ended up handling it differently. At recess and lunch break and after school when we could, we would talk about what we knew about gayness and the gay community. One of my friends brought gay pornographic magazines that he said he found; the other brought *The Advocate*, which was to become a well-known (inter)national LGBTQ+ magazine, but in the 1970s was primarily found in southern California and was geared toward gay male sexuality with plentiful and specific personal ads. One of the topics the three of us discussed incessantly was 'queers' (which has been reclaimed in contemporary times but was still a slur in the late sixties). We couldn't stop speculating and turning over the occasional news story, but we never admitted to having these feelings ourselves. We didn't quite trust each other yet. We did, however, talk about God. Noah, the boy I started bonding with in first year high school, didn't really care what God thought because he was proud to call himself an atheist. I and Michael, who started high school with us in second year, were both were scandalised by this frank declaration. Michael took a different tack from me. He believed in God but also believed, as his parents had taught him, that God was all loving and did not hate or punish the way we were being taught in religion class, where he was jeered at for being 'the guy with the kind God'. This didn't bother him in the least, and consequently he had a much more comfortable coming out a few years later. I, on the other hand, believed the priests who said that God hated me, and this made my own coming out more difficult. I kept my feelings bottled up inside me until I thought I would explode.

The formative moment for my own becoming occurred the summer between my second and third years of high school. I managed to buy a copy of *The Advocate*, which, as I said, was famous for its personal ads. Goaded on by my burgeoning sexual feelings – and to get it over with to see if I really was gay – I answered an ad placed by someone saying he wished to be a 'big brother to teen boys up to 16'. I wrote him a letter with my phone number, and he called me. We arranged to meet in front of a movie theater the following Saturday. Today I know this was reckless and dangerous; back then it was incredibly exciting and nerve-wracking. Not only did I meet him (with butterflies in my stomach), but I took him to our family home! (My second sister had married, and our parents were at our beach house.) Today I am ambivalent about the encounter: As a sexual experience it was at best mediocre, but the event taught me that I really was gay. Thus began at least six years of worrying, self-hatred, and despair. I didn't contemplate suicide as many teenagers do, but I was miserable and yet somehow excited to see what was next for me. I went to school the next year and proudly announced to Noah and Michael that I had 'done it!' Noah said he thought I was disgusting. Michael was sympathetic and told me privately that he had experimented too. We started going out together apart from Noah and started becoming intimate with each other, as best we could in a car! At one point we started going out on double dates with two girls he knew, and after we had dropped them off we would go somewhere and fool around with each other. Michael and I became 'best friends'. As I look back on it now, I realise he and I did the equivalent of 'going steady'. The last year of high school and first year of college we were inseparable, as he went to UCLA also.

During the summer between high school and college, Michael and I went on a cruise with my parents. It turned out to be a watershed time, inasmuch as we were extremely popular, especially with the ship's entertainers, while my parents were seemingly oblivious. Meanwhile I was making new friends and working part time. The mental/emotional/spiritual parts of myself were taken up with a two-fold dilemma. I've come to see the two parts as interrelated. First, during my last year of high school, I stopped going to church because I felt that if God hated me, there was no point. Moreover, my sexual encounters felt right to me. I imagined that if they were morally horrible they would not bring me so much pleasure and fulfilment. If the religious gatekeepers were to be believed, I should have been struck dead or otherwise corporally punished. Second, my relationship with my father was improving (the subject of which would require at least one essay of its own), even though he would continue to deride me for not being manly or interested in sports. I grappled with whether to tell my parents about my sexual orientation, but decided not to, based on what turned out to be wrong advice from my sister. My answer to the two-fold dilemma was to once again immerse myself in academics, so that I could prove to myself and others that I could excel and be successful at something while I retained outsider status from church and society.

I also wanted to be a success at being a gay man! In the 1970s this meant, from my own narrow perspective, drinking as much as possible, taking drugs whenever they were offered to me, and having as much sex as possible. While I was living with my parents, my activities were limited to one-night stands and anonymous encounters. After I got my own apartment in Hollywood at age twenty-three, however, I was able not only to continue this on a broader scale but also have people over, begin dating, and actually have a boyfriend. The question of God was not really present in my life. I envied those I knew who had long term relationships but didn't know how to find one. All things considered, I was pretty happy. I had a job I enjoyed, a nice apartment, some friends, and family I saw as often as I cared to. I was learning about true gayness from other gay men rather than Catholic priests and nuns and books and magazines.

When I was twenty-five, things changed for me. I became ill and had to curtail my going out for about two months. In COVID times this seems like nothing, but back then it was quite something. I read a great deal and watched a lot of television. How lucky we are now to have DVDs, the internet, and streaming video. During my time at home I wondered if there was something missing.

I realised there was when, the first night I was able to go out again, I met a young man who invited me to go to church with him! I didn't really want to, but I did want to see him again, so I agreed. He was keen on a church that reached out specifically to gays and lesbians. (We weren't LGBTQ+ yet by any means.) We went to that church, and I began a new phase of my journey. I may have heard before that God loved me (Michael certainly had stressed it enough), but that day I heard it from a woman who was ordained clergy, pastor of the church, and wearing the vestments I was used to seeing male priests wear. When she said that God loved me not in spite of being gay but *because* I was gay, it was an epiphany for me. Over the next few years I learned more about myself and who God could be for me. This church was a denomination called the Metropolitan Community Churches (MCC), and I remained an active member for longer than I had been in the Catholic Church. Through this church I learned that I was allowed – required actually – to question my faith journey.

As a result of my questioning, I decided to study theology and biblical interpretation. I entered the clergy training program and was ordained, received advanced degrees, pastored five churches over the course of thirty years, taught at the seminary level, and published scholarly texts and articles. I have been able to include my family in my life in a new way, as equals each on a spiritual journey that does not have to be the same to be fulfilling. Once I was comfortable with myself and who I was, coming out to my parents was quite easy and affirming. We became good friends and remained so until the day they died.

I am officially retired as clergy now, but I continue to question and seek and write. I am alarmed at the rise of the Christian Right and find that even the most liberal Christians tend to be too conservative for me. This is where feminism has been instrumental for me. When I studied for the ministry in the mid-eighties, feminism was beginning to be talked about in religious studies. I had teachers who exposed me to feminist works of theology, philosophy, and biblical interpretation, which has informed my own queer thoughts in these areas. Feminism has confirmed that questioning is essential and that everyone deserves a place at the table. One of my professors, lesbian feminist theologian Carter Heyward, always asked us, 'Who are we leaving out?', and this is a question I have been asking myself, my congregants, and my own students for many years. I learned that there is no hierarchy of oppressions: we are all in the struggle together toward establishing a world of right relations with self, others, and the earth.

One of the many gifts of feminism for me is the notion of 'Wholeness'. I have learned that we have diverse parts to our lives – physical, mental, emotional, and spiritual. Each of these must be nourished and balanced in order for us to be whole people. When we are out of balance, we create and empower dysfunction and unnecessary drama. We are not only ill at ease, we are dis/eased. We are strangers in our bodies; our emotions are in an uproar; our minds wander unhealthily; and our spirits are lifeless. What is missing when we are out of balance? Some would answer Christ; others would say God; still others would suggest diet and exercise; and finally some would say medication and therapy. My answer, based on my experience, is Authenticity. We must be authentic people in order to be whole people. This means taking a hard look at ourselves, loving ourselves, monitoring and changing ourselves when we need to. My early years were cluttered with other people's mandates of what was authentic – as a male child, as a Catholic, as a 'queer' (slur) and as a queer (post-slur). As long as I was tyrannised by Christianity, heteropatriarchy, heteronormativity, gender expectations, and even homonormativity, I was unable to be who I was intended to be.

For quite a while I was conflicted about leaving the Catholic Church. At this point in my life (post-retirement) I am conflicted about whether to remain with Christianity and make the best of it, heteropatriarchal warts and all. Nevertheless, I am firm and affirmed in my requirement of personal, queer authenticity. What about the other side of the (non)relationship? How do others feel about my choices? In the grand scheme of things, in my case at least, I don't think it matters to the institution at all. For example, I have clergy colleagues whose philosophy about people leaving the church is that 'for every one who leaves, two more will come', and they pass this along to their congregants. On a personal note, I don't think that Cardinal Joseph Ratzinger (the recently deceased self-styled 'Pope Emeritus', Benedict XVI) gave a damn that I and countless gay men left Catholicism, inasmuch as he constructed the theology that homosexuals are 'objectively disordered' and hence denied salvation. (Note: While the current pope, Francis I, has proffered love toward all people, he has not overruled this pronouncement.)

I am reminded of when Maya Angelou spoke of seeing someone at a party with whom she had had a falling out. She related that the other person was having a wonderful time and not giving Maya a thought, making her realise that she had wasted time and energy and unnecessary emotion allowing this person to inhabit her head, heart, and soul rent-free for years. Likewise, I believe I allowed others to occupy my inward parts rent-free while I worried about having left the church. Once I recognised that Spirit was not synonymous with any one religion or person or system of ethics, I became free and happy. Once my sexuality and my spirituality were in sync, I began to be in balance and whole. Consequently, my coming out to my family was a lot less stressful than it could have been. While I obsessed about the Church's position, I would have presented my sexuality in an angry way; but, once I realised this was who God had created me to be, I approached coming out as a sharing of myself and this was how my parents received it. As a matter of fact, they told me they had always known but didn't want to intrude. They had checked out the new church I was attending, afraid that I had joined a cult. They were happy if I was happy, and we remained actual friends until the day they died. My sister who remained within Catholicism has shared with me that many modern Catholics think for themselves on issues like abortion and same-sex marriage. So it's been a journey for us all.

∽

Today as I look out at the horizon of my life at the age of sixty-seven, I feel that in some ways, even though I left the Catholic Church, I did not cease being a Catholic. Many of my beliefs are still the same, but I have integrated them — and continue to do so every day — with my sexual personhood. In order to maintain what I call a sense/state of Queer Authenticity, I must be authentic to the Gay/Queer Person the Source of All has created me to be. No one else speaks for God. I discover God (whatever It is/They are) on my own terms. For me, God is Love, and whatever contradicts Love is not of God. In this regard, like some feminists, I think I am probably post-Christian now that I am not preaching from the Jewish and Christian scriptures every week. The rituals and the texts seem too confining now: they don't pass the 'sniff test' for authenticity for me any longer. I remember those who have taken steps on the journey with me, especially Noah and Michael, my parents, and that woman pastor who dared to tell me God loved me – all of whom have gone to their next journey before me. I doubt I will be able to read all of the books I have stockpiled over the years, and that's something I'm trying to make peace with, along with my ongoing physical maladies. In the meantime, I find beauty and joy in a philosophical discussion with my husband, in the twentieth viewing of the film *The Hours*, or in a delicious meal or a wonderfully dirty martini. If all of this makes my journey that of an apostate, I am definitely on for the full ride!

The Journey of a Misfit

Anthony Bash

As I have reflected on what to write, I have become aware that three themes run through my life. The principal one is that I feel, and to some extent I am, a misfit. This may partly be because I am likely to be at the moderate end of the autistic spectrum. One of my children has been diagnosed as being on the spectrum. At one of the assessments for our child (now an adult) my wife and I were asked to attend as parents to answer some questions about our child. It became clear from the questions and our answers to them that I too was 'ticking the boxes' for being on the spectrum. Second, coupled with the feeling of being a misfit is my sense of wanting to be accepted, mainstream, and ordinary. I do not like the feeling of being 'on the edge' and never quite with the in-crowd. Last, I am also something of an idealist, who has difficulty living comfortably with the pragmatic and even unpopular decisions we make (or experience) in life when we are part of communities and organisations.

I come from a secular Jewish family. On my late father's side, the family has been in Britain since at least the eighteenth century, and there are records of one distant relative who fought at the Battle of Trafalgar. My mother's family are from what is now Poland; they fled the pogroms of the early twentieth century. I am the first in our family to have gone to university, though my mother and my late father are clearly bright and able people. I was circumcised, in keeping with Jewish traditions, and was *bar mitzvah* when aged thirteen. I learned Hebrew up till then, and after my *bar mitzvah*, I did not go back to a synagogue until my grandmother's funeral fifteen years later.

What I recall feeling up to the age 13, when I stopped going to synagogue, was the mismatch between what I read and heard in the Old Testament and the practices of those I saw around me. 'If this is faith and religion,' I thought, 'it is not for me.' I saw what I regarded as double standards: holding to the form of religious faith but with none of the practices transformed by the power of religious faith. I do not doubt my observations were partly over-critical and immature, but I suspect there was a basis of truth to them, for some expressions of Judaism can be predominantly about culture and traditions, as they were for my parents, rather than about an active, lived out faith that touches cognition, affect, and behaviour. Of course, this perception may partly be a case of 'beams' in one's own eye and 'specks' in others' eyes, and the immaturity of pre-adulthood.

Despite what I observed, I was hungry for what I would now call 'spiritual truth.' My teens were lonely years. I was a misfit at school, and I did not make friends or like sport, parties, or the music of the 'swinging sixties'. I spent time reading. I had a sense that there was more to life than the material world, and I discovered through what I read some of the yearnings of others. I could not have named what those yearnings were, but I knew I shared them, and that I had an inner restlessness to find out more. I was fascinated by the writings of C. G. Jung; the poems of William Wordsworth and T. S. Eliot captivated me; I read Dante's *Inferno* and was deeply moved. I had a teacher at school who, in hindsight, was clearly a Christian, though at the time I did not fully appreciate that. What I do recall is that he was different from other people in an attractive way. I was looking for something, and I knew I would recognise it when I found it.

I went to Bristol University when aged eighteen and came across what we called the 'God Squad'. They were keen, well-meaning Christians who seemed to me to be odd and spineless. I thought they had a dogmatic approach to life that was irrelevant to me and to what I was thinking. Having said that, I remember the Junior Common Room President when I arrived at the Hall of Residence where I stayed. His life and conduct were different. He made me feel that I wanted to be like him. I later discovered he was a Christian, and I was (in my youthful arrogance) surprised that someone could be a Christian and such a charismatic, engaging person. I am still in touch with him, more than half a century later, and we exchange Christmas cards each year.

I had, in truth, one good friend, while I was at school. He too was Jewish, and from a secular family, without the sort of yearnings I had for what I would now call 'spiritual reality'. He went to university and after a few months started writing to me – yes, these were the days long before email, when people communicated with distant friends by hand-written letters – to say he had started to experience strange phenomena he could not explain according to his previous mindset. I suspected at once that the 'God Squad' had got hold of him and, if I was right, I determined that I would 'de-convert' him to bring back to unbelief an otherwise lost soul.

We met in the Easter vacation of that year, and I could see the palpable change in his life. I doubt that he will read this, but I can say (and I would not mind if he did read it) that he had been a rather arrogant, full-of-himself person. What I now saw was someone who was changing. It seemed to me like an organic change, rather than a new pattern of behaviour he had decided to adopt.

I expressed my dismay that he had been 'got' by the 'God Squad'. He astonished me by saying that he believed in a physical resurrection of Jesus Christ, and then asked me, 'If you were persuaded that Jesus did rise from the dead, would you believe it?' The question, of course, trapped me: intellectually, if the resurrection did happen, I would be constrained to believe it. However, I was confident it was not true, and so I would not have to believe it. I determined to 'cure' my friend of his foolishness, since (or so I thought) we all know that dead people stay dead and do not rise again.

Without going into detail, the next few months were tumultuous for me because very much against my will, I became persuaded, as I read and thought about the historicity of the resurrection, that the resurrection did happen as an event in history. This confidence has not left me, and I remain unpersuaded by the speculative alternatives that some academic theologians suggest. During this period. I also read parts of the New Testament for the first time and was captivated by the living Jesus I met in the Gospel of John. Eventually, I gave up resisting what I knew was true. I remember thinking that my view had formerly been that Christians were like ostriches: they stuck their heads in sand to ignore what would otherwise lead them to unbelief. I realised I was the ostrich, with my own head in sand because I did not want to face up to the truth of the historicity of the resurrection. So, in the summer of 1972, I stopped resisting what I had come to see was true and gave in to what I would now say is the call of Christ. I have just passed the half-century of that time. I was then aged twenty.

What was I to say to my parents? I waited five months before saying anything. In the Christmas vacation of that year, I told my father first. He was aghast and deeply disappointed with me. I then told my mother – against my father's express wish – who went to bed and cried for a week. To my parents, it was as if I had renounced my heritage and background and despised the sacrifice of Jewish people who had died in the Second World War and in earlier pogroms. My parents barely spoke to me for the following twenty years. It was only when I started to go out with Melanie, who is now my wife, that my parents once again 'owned' their son, and, later to their immense credit, welcomed my Gentile wife into the family.

Shortly after I became a Christian, I started to worship at Christchurch, Clifton, in Bristol, where Paul Berg was vicar. I regard Paul as one of the great unsung clergy of the twentieth century. He used to have a saying that has stuck with me over the years and which I often quote. He would say of his faith, 'I am sure I have got 95 per cent of the truth of Christianity right. The only trouble is, I do not know which 5 per cent I have got wrong.' Personally, I am not so confident to say I have got as much as '95 per cent of the truth of Christianity right'. What I would say is that I do not know how much I have got wrong. I suspect it is more than 5 per cent.

Paul Berg's pragmatic attitude to his own convictions has helped me to recognise the provisional nature of what Christians believe and it has given me the freedom to rethink my faith as I have matured or learned more. This has sometimes been to the disquiet of those around me. They regard me as a 'waverer' about what I think and believe, lacking in conviction and confidence. To my mind, this is simply not true. Some writers and editors of each of the Old Testament and the New Testament lived in a no-man's land of questioning while still holding on to the core of their faith. 'Qoheleth' in Ecclesiastes and Job are obvious examples; so too is John the Baptist when in prison. We ignore the integrity of their examples at our peril.

Over the years, I have added to what Paul Berg said. It seems to me that, in one sense, the Bible is no more than ink on the page – a series of letters forming units that we call 'words' and 'sentences'. They are a cipher than requires an interpretive key to be understood. I do believe that Scripture is God-breathed; however, God has not given human beings the key to the cipher. I put it like this: God has given us the inspired Scriptures, but not an inspired hermeneutic. In other words, how we interpret the Scriptures is 'up for grabs,' and there is not a necessarily right way to read the texts. This gives each generation great freedom to interpret for itself what it reads, and not to be shackled or constrained by the interpretations of the past. So, for example, although the pre-medieval Church Fathers may have believed a particular something about Christian truth, this does not mean that Christians in the twenty-first century are constrained to hold the same view or interpretation.

To hold such views is to be in both an uncomfortable and a liberating place. It is also one that is not necessarily popular, because one may end up challenging or questioning 'the received view' or 'the view of the church'. I find myself 'in' the church and also sometimes not 'of' it because I want to be less dogmatic and authoritarian about what I believe than some people in the church would want me to be. I seek space to explore and doubt, and space to disagree. I may hold this or that view today; tomorrow, I may have changed my mind. In short, I do not fit in a box. I believe things from a range of disparate traditions and outlooks. To be in such a place can be lonely.

A Lutheran view of Paul and his conversion very much prevailed when I first became a Christian: this is the view that Paul was burdened by legalism and a works-based approach to salvation. The approach is supposedly typical of the Old Testament and is supposedly also typical of Jewish people as well as Catholic Christianity. Those who hold such a view say that Paul was 'converted' when he realised that salvation was by grace through faith alone. Well-meaning people warned me when I first became a Christian to renounce Judaism's 'works-based' attempts at righteousness, and to beware all things Jewish as they could shipwreck my new-found faith. The warnings were meant well, as they were based on a reading of the New Testament that was then widespread. I say more about this below.

In my thirties I left the practice of law as a solicitor and worked with students and other young people in Glasgow for a para-church organisation that was very much rooted in the conservative evangelicalism of the United States. Sadly, I have since fallen out with the para-church organisation over its rigid approach to the Bible. I was deeply grieved, for example, by the way the organisation treated a friend. I was grieved because of what I understood to be the organisation's naive and even heartless interpretation of the Bible in relation to my friend and his family.

Where I worshipped in Glasgow was shaped by the evangelical conservatism of a certain branch of the Church of Scotland. I was reasonably comfortable in that setting, but I continued to think independently within other frameworks of thought I then inhabited. However, I was always 'on the edge' because I knew I did not fit with what most people said and thought. I kept distance enough, with the result that few knew of the debates about faith and Christian doctrines that I was having with myself. However, I eventually left the church where I attended after the minister preached a sermon which was clearly critical of what I had said in an unexceptional conversation with him earlier that week. I think he hoped I would be smitten with guilt and shame by what he intended as a covert, public rebuke. Perhaps immaturely, I just grinned as I listened to the sermon – astonished at what I took to be his audacity and gall – and never went back to the church.

My years in Scotland were profoundly influential on my

future development. While working with the para-church organisation, I took a beginners' New Testament Greek class at a local Bible College. Starting to read the New Testament in Greek opened a new world of thought to me, and I began to understand the New Testament beyond the grid of mainstream translations. It is not that the translations are wrong; it is that starting to read the New Testament in Greek helped me to think in new ways about what I was reading and to make connections that are not obvious in English translations. After I had completed the Greek course, I started a degree in theology at Glasgow University. I am not exaggerating when I say that the degree was profoundly life-changing for me for at least three reasons.

The first is that I met academic theologians including John Riches, John Barclay, Robert Davidson, and Christopher Evans. I had been warned that academic theologians and their thought would be dangerous and destructive for faith. However, I quickly came to see that many of them were people of deep faith who thought 'out of the box' of the sort of traditions I sometimes inhabited. They were asking questions and living with open-ended uncertainties that did not destroy their faith. I am deeply grateful, for example, to the late Robert Davidson whose book, *The Courage to Doubt*, and his Old Testament theology course, taught me to ask questions and to recognise that the Bible is full of people who were asking questions and who did not know the answers. The Bible became to me a book of lively debate about the core of their faith, about what that faith meant, and how it could be expressed and lived out. In the churches and Christian organisations of which I have been part, I had not met many others with the same outlook. And now, though I say the creeds and affirm that they represent aspects of my faith, I sometimes say to myself, 'I wish there were footnotes clarifying and nuancing what is there.'

Secondly, a book written by Geza Vermes, *Jesus the Jew*, became widely read, and – I am slightly embarrassed to write this, though I was then 'a child of my times' – through it I came to see that Jesus was Jewish, that most of the people who wrote the New Testament were Jewish, and that being a Christian was to follow the teachings of a sect of Judaism started by Jesus and developed further by Paul.

Through this then-new understanding (now mainstream), I became comfortable with the idea that I was from a Jewish background, and I did not need to treat my background as something of a 'secret' of my past that was not to play a part in my present life. I also realised that embracing my Jewish identity was not a threat to my faith or to believing and practising the central doctrines of Christianity. Though I would now describe myself as a 'Jewish Christian', very few people in the Jewish community would regard me as Jewish, and I am regarded with suspicion by members of my parents' Jewish family. I belong, but not in their view. There are also some contemporary Jewish-Christians who do not agree with the limited way I express my Jewish identity in the day-to-day way I worship and live.

Third, I was deeply influenced by the writings of the late E. P. Sanders whose books on Paul were being published in the 1970s and 1980s. Sanders's work is now regarded as mainstream in academic circles, though developed and refined by later theologians. Briefly, Sanders challenged the Lutheran view of Paul. This is the view that Paul was troubled by the 'weight' of his sins until he realised that salvation was not by doing good or by self-effort but by God's gift of grace through faith. Sanders showed, as had a few others before him, that Judaism was as much a religion of grace and faith as Christianity, and that Paul was interpreting his Christian experience in the light of his understanding of *Jewish* theology. To summarise Sanders, it is not that Paul was encumbered by sin and was looking to good works to cancel the debt of sin; rather, Paul was flourishing as a Jew and realised that Jesus, and not the law, or good deeds, or the Jewish covenant, was the answer to the human condition. Paul then sought to explore and explain what it was that Jesus was the answer to. Sanders put it this way memorably: Paul moved 'from solution to plight' and not (as in mainstream Protestant thought) the other way round.

As a result of learning Greek and studying theology, I felt as if I was in a new world of thought. It was a world of thought that was nourishing and deepening my faith, not destroying it. Alas, many of those around me did not have the same privileges as I, and increasingly I felt I did not belong. It is not that I was ejected, expelled, or excluded; it is that outside the academic community, I felt very much alone. Some did look on and regard my growth and development as a lamentable falling away from the 'true path' of faith and discipleship.

I went on to study for a PhD in New Testament in Cambridge, and the experience further deepened my sense of inner freedom in and through the Scriptures, though I continued to feel increasingly isolated from some of the mainstream expressions of Christian faith. I once said to my supervisor, Morna Hooker, that I no longer knew where I belonged in the spectrum of the expressions of Christianity. I told her that I was not a fundamentalist, and that those who called themselves 'liberals' or 'evangelicals' would not see me as 'one of them'. 'Well,' said Morna, 'why don't you call yourself 'a Christian'?' She then added, 'After all, this was good enough for St Luke.' I was put in my place, and then, as on so many other occasions, I benefited from her wisdom and clarity of mind.

While in Cambridge, I worshipped in a church where I met (and later married) Melanie. I was becoming increasingly frustrated with what I felt was the naivety and confessional dogmatism of the church. I found listening to the sermons particularly difficult. I used to take a Greek New Testament when we went to services in the church. After months of irritation and to stop myself becoming exasperated with what I was hearing, I read the Greek New Testament during the sermons, instead of listening. Melanie later told me she used to think, 'What a godly man I have married: he sits there and reads the New Testament lectionary passages in Greek.' I was well and truly rumbled when the sermon one week was on the Old Testament reading, and yet I still read my Greek New Testament oblivious to the incongruity of doing so.

I met Martyn Percy while I was studying for my PhD. He was already ordained. He invited me to stay for a weekend with him and Emma, his wife, who was also ordained. They were curates in a church in Bedford, and they modelled a freedom of thought and faith within a different Christian tradition from the one I knew. I found them and their inner freedom hugely attractive, and that weekend visit played a significant part in leading me to explore ordination in later months and years. I learned that weekend that there were other ways of vibrant ministry outside the sort of straight-jacketed evangelicalism that I was used to. Martyn and Emma remain good friends and an important, continuing influence on me.

I am now an ordained minister of the Church of England and (with the one exception I refer to below) have thrived for the decade I was in parish ministry. Even so, I only just 'made it' to ordination. At the end of my first year, a member of staff at the theological college I was at wrote to my diocese saying (in effect) I was unsuitable for ordination. I later learned that other staff at the college, as well as the bishop of the diocese from which I came, disagreed. Four months later, a report on me to the diocese written by another member of staff said the opposite to what had previously been said. I have smiled to myself since then that in the space of four months I had apparently changed so profoundly.

After I left the college and was ordained, two of the College staff informally told me that, in their view, the member of staff who wrote so critically about me sometimes took an undeserved and irrational hostility towards one or two of the students at the college. They also thought that the member of staff had attributed the severe pregnancy sickness from which Melanie had suffered in her second pregnancy (as she has in all three of her pregnancies) to mental ill-health that somehow rendered *me* unsuitable for ordination. I do not know whether these 'off the record' statements are true; they certainly made sense of my experience. When I told all this to a bishop in the Diocese where I was ordained, he looked unsurprised and said, 'Welcome to the Church of England.'

I have thrived best in churches that do not have a strong confessional and partisan identity. This has given me the freedom to allow the Scriptures to speak to me and, I hope, to speak through me when I preach. At different times, I have also been an Anglican chaplain at Durham University in two of the colleges. It saddened me to know that the more evangelical churches in Durham warned students to avoid me and the college chapels because I was a danger to 'sound faith'. I took it as a compliment when one student said to me, after two years of attending lectures I gave, that though he had been warned otherwise, he had realised I had a real, living, and passionate faith and that the lectures had helped to open his mind and had deepened his own faith.

At one stage of my ministerial career, I was Team Rector in a newly formed team of six parishes. At my welcoming service, one of the churchwardens in the most recently included church in the Team told me plainly that the church did not want to be in the Team. I also had to adjourn the second PCC meeting I chaired at one of the churches because several members were shouting at me. I said from the outset that I wanted to be more than a chaplain to declining congregations with the task of managing the decline. The hostility towards me was astonishing. Senior clergy got involved and despite 'closed-door meetings' without me present, no one could find a reason to require me to leave. I was even offered a 'sweetener' (this was the word that was used) if I agreed to leave. I declined it. I felt deeply unsupported in seeking no more than to carry out what the ordinal required me to do. In the end, it was Melanie who, after eighteen months in the Team, persuaded me to leave, due to the increasing amount of stress I was under.

As I reflect on my ministerial career, which for the majority of the time has not been in parish ministry but in a university setting, I wonder how much the Church of England values its principal resources – its parish clergy. Time and money were spent to 'discern my call' and to give me and my growing family support for two years of residential training. More money was spent in the years following ordination on what is called 'Initial Ministerial Education'. Yet I was edged out of a parish to look for work outside the 'core business' of the Church. It appears that this was done without thought about retaining and redeploying someone the Church had trained and invested in. No one helped me to discern a supposed call to leave. Anecdotal evidence suggests that a sizeable number of those who are initially in residential ministerial training do not remain in parish ministry but, like me, leave for related but not parish-based work. I do not think this is 'value for money' for the Church's investment in people or value for money for the people who give sacrificially to the ministry of the Church.

I suspect I am not regarded in the Church as a 'safe pair of hands' because, in the words of a friend of mine, I sometimes 'rattle the bars of the cage'. For this reason and because I have not sought to climb what another friend of mine has called 'the greasy pole of preferment' in the Church, I have not been offered opportunities to contribute nationally to the Church of England's reflections on questions to do with forgiveness, repentance, and reconciliation. These questions have been a central part of my academic work for the last twenty-five years. In my view, what I have written about and explored are both relevant to and even significant for some of the issues the Church of England is facing. Of course, on my part there may be an inflated view of the significance and relevance of the contribution I could make. Nevertheless, I am left with a sense that the work has been side-lined, not taken seriously, and not noticed because I have not 'ticked the right boxes' or been in the right theological 'clubs'.

Theologically, how do I make sense of all of this? My lack of a contribution institutionally and my sense of isolation and of not belonging may lie at the heart of what it means to be a Christian and of the vocation of being a Christian. It is unexceptional to say that to be a Christian is to be a follower of Jesus Christ. Whether one is called to serve at the core of an institution such as a church or in a more peripheral role, one is always an outsider, a critic, something of a prophet who challenges the status quo. Whatever and wherever the role and place of the calling, it will sometimes be lonely, isolated, and isolating. The longing that I have – the longing to belong and to stop being a misfit – can be reframed as being something of the typical experience of those who are Christians. Christians are *called* to be misfits – not to be 'conformed to this world' (as Paul says in Romans 12:2) – and part of the counter-cultural kingdom of God that reverses so much of what we otherwise take as axiomatic. Of course, this is lonely and highlights that the Christian's belonging is above all to Christ. The state of not belonging is the proper condition and the vocation of the Christian. But it does not excuse, fully explain, or justify institutional neglect or (in the tragic experience of some) even abuse.

From Exclusive to Inclusive

Ian S. Markham

Looking back on my life, there are several very different 'me' personas. Over my sixty years, among my many personas, I have been a fundamentalist Christian in one season and a liberal Christian in a different one. Interestingly, in each season I was utterly committed to the truth of my beliefs. I tended to be puzzled why others were not so persuaded. There is a mystery in conversion. I am not sure how and why one journeys from one worldview to another.

Persona one: the fundamentalist child
Starting with my fundamentalist worldview, the genesis is easy to identify. Perhaps everyone is born into a worldview. In 1962, I was born into what others call 'The Exclusive Brethren'. The Exclusives are a subset of the Plymouth Brethren, which was founded in the 1820s. Interestingly, the founders broke away from the Anglican Church. They wanted to re-create the simplicity of the New Testament church: Christians were just Christians; everyone was a saint; and all believers were priests; titles like 'reverend' did not exist; the key service was the 'Lord's Supper', and worship patterns were simple and

were led by the Holy Spirit, not read out of a book.

In 1848 the movement split in two. There was a doctrinal disagreement over whether or not Jesus was *able* to sin. Benjamin Wills Newton of Plymouth thought, among other claims, that, although Jesus did not sin, Jesus was able to sin. John Nelson Darby of Bristol disagreed. A governance disagreement ensued. The so-called 'Open Brethren' wanted each assembly to have its own jurisdiction over its members; John Nelson Darby (1800-1882) wanted all assemblies to be of 'one heart and one mind.' At this moment, Darby birthed the 'Exclusive Brethren'.

By 1962, the Exclusives were shaped by the dispensationalist theology of Darby: zealous preoccupation with eschatology and, in particular, the imminent return of our Lord in the rapture; deep suspicion of ecumenism (after all, the *one* church is one of the signs of the end), and passionate support for the state of Israel. The rapture was a preoccupation. I remember when I was recovering from the flu at the age of seven, getting out of bed, walking around an empty house, increasingly convinced that I had been 'left behind.' When my mother came in from the outside yard where she had been hanging out the washing, she held me close while I continued to sob about my fear that I had been left behind. During my childhood, I gave my life to Jesus repeatedly to ensure that I was not one of those who had been left behind.

Although separation from the world was always a theme, it took a greater intensity under the leadership of James Taylor Junior. As a child, 'separation from the world' took the form of never inviting a friend into my house, television and cinema being forbidden, meetings to study the Bible every night, services starting at 6am on Sunday morning, limited access to technology, and a prohibition on joining anything except the Body of Christ (so trade unions, voluntary civic organisations were all forbidden).

For me, one gift of this childhood environment is that one never doubts the reality of God. The reality of God is an assumption: it is the primary operating principle of all living and life. Perhaps because of that intensity of upbringing, my sense of the presence of God has remained inescapable. There have been seasons where I wish it were not so – seasons when I wanted to be an atheist. But it was impossible. Even after my mother died when I was 19 and I was angry with God, God was there. I prayed despite my desire not to pray.

For a conversion to happen, there does need to be some type of sociological shift. If this worldview had been left undisturbed, the chances are I would have stayed in the Exclusive Brethren, found a line of work, and settled into the patterns of living that my parents had. However, it all changed when I was eight and my father ran into a major problem with the prohibition on civic organisations.

Legislation was introduced in the late 1960s that required all pharmacists to be members of the Pharmaceutical Society. My father stopped practising as a pharmacist and attempted to become a supplier of chemist sundries to pharmacy shops. With six children to feed, he realised that he was not earning enough to support his family. Bankruptcy was looming. His dilemma was acute: both bankruptcy and membership in the Pharmaceutical Society were incompatible with membership of the Exclusive Brethren.

I still marvel at the decision he made. He took the brave decision to leave the Exclusive Brethren. The concluding correspondence with my grandfather and uncle is all focused on the repayment of debts (it was the practice for loans to be made within the fellowship rather than with a bank). His brother Roy wrote to my father:

The amount I supplied is 2,820 pounds. I am glad you are able to see the way clear to settle most of your outstanding debts. ... I notice you hope to pay at least 270 pounds on the sale of your house. This arrangement will be quite satisfactory if you are remaining in the fellowship, but if not, then I must ask you to clear the loan as quickly as possible.

I remember being with my father as he called his siblings, and the financial dimension of the decision was a key part of the conversation. The consequences were brutal. As a family, every single person that we knew in the universe would never speak to us again. For the Exclusives, those who had 'seen the light and then rejected it' are most condemned. No one would have any contact with us.

Apart from one telegram informing my father than my grandfather had passed and an exchange of letters with his brother Paul in 2003, there was no further contact between my father and his family. The exchange of letters between my uncle Paul and my father reveals the theology:

Uncle Paul wrote:

With sorrow I note how your family is so connected with the world where Jesus was cast out. However we must be thankful there must be some testimony to the Lord Jesus by those you baptised in faith that God would work in them. The Lord Jesus 'ever lives to make intercession for us' even when we have strayed from the path which leads to life.

You have had contact with brethren with whom you were once local and who walk in separation to the Truth. This communication need not be prolonged. I write with the earnest concern that the time remaining may be in true enjoyment of the fellowship of God's Son Jesus Christ our Lord (1 Cor 1 v 9). You once enjoyed this and only the Holy Spirit can bring conviction of the Truth thus experienced.

The letter concludes with the simple words, '*Your own brother, Paul*'.

It is an interesting letter. The confidence that the Exclusives had 'the Truth' is absolute. Even now, the brother's implied plea to my father was 'repent and return'.

Perhaps shaped by these assumptions, the Exclusives' world view lingered in my family for many more years. After all, my parents had been in the Exclusives for over forty years; their departure was more pragmatic than principled. They were still persuaded of the dangers of the world, the apostasy of the mainline churches, and of the fact that we are living in the last days.

For a time, we lived in the twilight world of the ex-members of the Exclusives. We would meet in the home of another former member for the breaking of the bread on Sunday morning. Then over time, we found an Open Brethren assembly, which was very conservative. These ostensibly 'open brethren' were opposed to all ecumenical projects, had strict expectations of behaviour, and continued to teach and stress an apocalyptic worldview. It was in this environment, at the age of twelve, that I became a boy preacher.

Persona two: the fundamentalist in the world

A factor in conversion must be simply growing up. As a child in an Exclusives' universe (whether in full communion or in the twilight world), there is little room for alternative worldviews. But as one enters one's teenage years, where differentiation from your parents is inevitable, interesting alternatives start emerging.

I found plenty of helpful apologists who reassured me about my fundamentalist faith. Josh McDowell's *Evidence that Demands a Verdict* (the latest edition was published in 2017) and Michael Green's *Runaway World* (1968) became key texts. With friends at my High School, I started CHAT (Christian Help Aid

Talk). Every week we invited speakers to talk to students at the school. Sometimes, with some nervousness, we even invited the occasional Anglican to address the group.

The key dynamic at work here was a fundamentalism in conversation with the world. I was utterly convinced of the mantra that 'the truth does not need to fear questions' – a mantra that my father often asserted. A key shift from persona one to persona two was the fact that I was permitted to study 'Religious Education' at High School.

A pause at this point is in order. In the United Kingdom, 'Religious Education' (RE) was required to be taught in schools since the Education Act of 1944. The Exclusives, exercised their legal right, and required members to withdraw their children from RE. So I never went to a RE class until we moved away from Devon in the UK (where I was born) to Cornwall (where my father became a pharmacist). In secondary school, I had an excellent RE teacher. John Keast had been trained at King's College London. He gently invited me to confront the complexities of Scripture. In countless classes we discussed inerrancy. How do you reconcile the different accounts of the death of Judas? Is it really plausible that God stopped the earth spinning (the only way to stop the sun) just to enable more people to be killed? How come in the Gospel of Mark Jesus talks endlessly about the Kingdom of God, but in the Gospel of Matthew it is the Kingdom of Heaven?

Now, at this point, I do want to insist that 'reason' is playing a role. However, I pause even here. Fundamentalist theologians can be academically very capable. Another thinker that fascinated me was Francis Schaeffer. His whole project, in books such as *The God Who Is There* (1968), sought to expose the manifest inconsistency of atheism and called for, as an alternative, a return to the classic Christian commitments of inerrancy in the Bible. Extremely intelligent people can defend with some rigor a range of positions. What appears reasonable to me can appear as less reasonable to someone else with comparable academic credentials.

But as I lived in these two worlds of fundamentalism and conversation, I found myself shifting. Even if I could imaginatively arrive at an explanation for the inconsistency in the biblical witness, I couldn't escape the reality that it certainly looks like there is in Scripture the 'appearance of error'. Why would God do that? At that point, it became easier to simply concede that there are factual and historical errors in Scripture. My second persona was slowly fading.

Persona three: Discovering Anglicanism

During my college applications, I was aware that there was a crucial moment. Encouraged by friends who belonged to a local Baptist Church, I applied to the London Bible College (now the London School of Theology) and also to King's College London. The London Bible College (LBC) was founded in 1943. This was an evangelical college, with a doctrinal statement that continues to affirm that the Scriptures are 'fully trustworthy in all that they affirm; and as the written Word of God they are our supreme authority for faith and conduct'. An alternative was King's College London. This was one of the colleges of the University of London. King's College London was founded in 1829. It had an Anglican foundation and an illustrious faculty and alumni who included F. D. Maurice (as Faculty) and Desmond Tutu (as an alumnus).

This moment of decision was crucial. I was choosing to be socialised in an Anglican, rather than in a non-Anglican environment. And I was making the decision without ever deciding to become an Anglican. Once again, I am not entirely sure what factors made me pick one over the other. Probably prestige was one: King's London was an elite university recognised throughout the world. But, more seriously, I knew that I was ready to leave the evangelical world. God's world was just much more complicated than the binary of 'saved' and 'damned' that dominates the fundamentalist narrative. The simple questions were the hardest: why are there so many religions if Christianity is the true one? Why does the Bible appear to err if the Bible is really inerrant? Why does God allow all these confusions?

One more factor was decisive. A biographical question was coming to the fore: how do we avoid religious intolerance? When my parents left the Exclusives, they were completely excluded. Their sin was the need to be employed and feed a family. A worldview that rejected a family for that sin was problematic. I knew that faith had to accommodate complexity, handle doubt, be gentle with the sinner, and find ways to be always in some type of relationship with one another and with God. A lifetime project was emerging at this time: how do you reconcile truth and toleration? This became the focus of my doctoral studies, which resulted in my book *Plurality and Christian Ethics* (1994). I decided the time had come to be socialised into the Anglican world.

My undergraduate years at King's College remain some of the happiest of my life. The boy from Bodmin, Cornwall (a small rural town) was living in London, the capital of the country. King's had a strong faculty. It was a thriving center of pioneering theology and religious studies. I learned from Leslie Houlden, Graham Stanton, Keith Ward, Colin Gunton, Michael Knibb, Colin Hickling, Brian Horne, Judith Maltby, Grace Jantzen, Stewart Sutherland, Richard Harries and Peter Byrne. Friendships that have lasted a lifetime were formed during those three years. And this was the moment when I became an Anglican.

Persona four: Getting confirmed as an Anglican

By the time I made the move to Anglicanism, I had already been baptised twice. In the Exclusives, they had infant baptism (after all, the biblical record in Acts has entire households being baptised); so my father had me baptised as a baby. When I became a member of a Baptist Church in a brief sojourn in Plymouth Devon, I was baptised as a believer. So, when the Revd Christopher Moody met with me about my confirmation as an Anglican, he decided that there was no need for me to be rebaptised.

The decision had been a complex mixture. First, there was this discovery of the significance of tradition. My fundamentalism tended to move straight from the Bible to the present-day Church. Creeds, as such, were not important. We appreciated that they were the summary of the biblical witness (in particular, the affirmation of the doctrine of the Trinity); but they were not central. We were the church that accepted Biblical authority. And on the whole, tradition was viewed with some suspicion: after all, there is no way that the Bible taught such concepts as the veneration of the Virgin Mary.

It was the simple question – originally asked by my RE teacher – that undermined this understanding of Biblical authority. 'Isn't it the case that the Church decided which books should go into the Bible?' John's Gospel was hotly debated; some of the initial lists of New Testament book included the Shepherd of Hermas. At the very least, I conceded that some authority for Christian truth needed to reside with the community of Christians. Anglicans recognise both Scripture and tradition (the witness of the Church through the ages) as authorities. My evangelical conviction that *sola scriptura* was sufficient felt implausible given the way the canon of the Bible was compiled.

Second, there was my growing love of the liturgy. For years, I had disparaged the scripted prayers that seemed to deny the agency of the Holy Spirit. Slowly I discovered that the Holy Spirit had been completely involved when those prayers were originally written down. I found the rhythm of the liturgy deeply powerful. I had been very critical that it was the same thing every service. But then the liturgy started going inside. I have reflected on the significance of liturgy in my essay in Joseph S. Pagano and Amy E. Richter, *Common Prayer: Reflections on Episcopal Worship* (Cascade 2020). Parts of this section on liturgy are taken from my essay in that book. In *Letters to Malcolm: Chiefly on Prayer* (1963), C. S. Lewis got it right when he explained what a worshipper wants out of a service:

> *They go to use the service, or, if you prefer, to* enact *it. Every service is a structure of acts and words through which we receive a sacrament, or repent, or supplicate, or adore. And it enables us to do these things best — if you like, it 'works' best — when, through long familiarity, we don't have to think about it. As long as you notice, and have to count, the steps, you are not dancing but only learning to dance. A good shoe is a shoe you don't notice. Good reading becomes possible when you need not consciously think about eyes, or light, or print, or spelling. The perfect church service would be one we're almost unaware of; our attention would have been on God.* (Original emphasis)

I sat through Morning Prayer; I attended the Eucharist. I learned the services inside out. They became a frame of reference in which I could pray, cry, and think in the presence of God. In the liturgy, I appreciated the centrality of the biblical text: the Book of Common Prayer is almost all scripture (although sometimes indirectly). I appreciated that the sermon was not doing the heavy lifting of the service; for the Office, it was the canticles; for the Eucharist, it was the Great Thanksgiving. It became a perfectly fitting shoe. I also knew where I was in the liturgy, even if a word or phrase had triggered a 'zoned out' moment where I offered some deep agony, some distracted thought, some hope or fear to God. The liturgy provided some space to work on my mind and my life. The twenty-two-year-old had found God's tools to work on his life.

My third and final reason is that I loved the space that Anglicanism provided for intellectual reflection and speculation. One of my favourite professors at King's College London was Leslie Houlden. He was often present in chapel. Yet he was also one of the so-called 'seven against Christ' – a contributor to *The Myth of God Incarnate*. I remember at the time being puzzled by how this distinguished progressive New Testament scholar could participate fully in the traditional Morning Office, almost all of which was Scripture. When I asked him this question, he responded by explaining that it is the very rhythm of the liturgy that gives him the freedom to question the tradition. It is the very certainty that the text brings him back to these ancient themes and prayers that permits him to reflect, question, and interrogate those themes and prayers.

In the Exclusives, there was no such intellectual freedom. As I have aged, a new persona is emerging. I am realising that in countless ways I want to affirm a 'conservative' account of the faith. Strangely, this word now simply means a person opposed to the full inclusion of LGBT+ persons. It is so odd, in my view, to define orthodoxy simply by one issue in sexual ethics (if ethics is the territory that determines conservative or liberal, then why not war or divorce?). By conservative, I mean a person who affirms the truth of the Incarnation, believes that the language of the Trinity captures something true about God, and thinks that angels or sacraments or priesthood might still mean something.

But as I find myself believing more and more every day, I am grateful that I am in the Anglican tradition where my company includes those who want to think in different ways about the nature and content of the faith.

In conclusion

I am still puzzled by the journey of conversion. What exactly is the relationship between 'truth' and my changing dispositions and outlooks as I journey through life? I take seriously the sociology of knowing. One's initial worldview is determined by birthplace and the dominant influences of parents. Then the combination of a teenager's healthy differentiation from one's parents, coupled with the many conversations with different ways to look at the world, creates a changing dynamic. Then one's decisions about 'company' (those I will let socialise me) is crucial. Rational reflection on the world is definitely a factor, although of course different people embark on the rational weighing of factors in different ways. So, perhaps, it is experience that is crucial: the prison of Exclusivism was replaced by the open system of Anglicanism, the unstructured informality of the Exclusivists has been replaced by the rhythm of the liturgy, and the wicked intolerance of Exclusivism has been replaced by a fear of prejudice that expresses itself as an inability to appreciate other viewpoints.

My kindred spirits, regardless of denomination or religion, tend to be those who believe yet hold their beliefs with some humility. I love the Nur tradition in Islam; I admire the Catholicism of Pope Francis; I even like the atheism of Alain de Botton, although he doesn't believe very much. How people carry their convictions matters to me. A gentleness and generosity in outlook, coupled with a commitment to conversation, are much needed.

From Exclusive to Inclusive

From my sixty-year-old vantage point, I am grateful for the twists and turns. And I am crucially grateful for the place I am in. I offer this moment to God and aspire to continue to be open to the truth that God will unfold in the continuing journey of life.

Embracing Grace

Rosemary Sempell

I remember a time in my late twenties when my brother accused me of having given up the faith of my forefathers! I disagreed and replied along the lines of, 'well thank goodness, as I would prefer hell to your version of God's love which was all too judgemental, fearful, and lacking in grace'. I recollect a few occasions around this time when I felt that he was trying to 'convert' me by explaining the error of my ways and saying how sinful I was because I was not maintaining what he knew to be the truth. This included a time when he visited with a fellow theological student and spent an evening preaching to me and some dinner guests. It ended with him saying he would 'pray for me'. He later assured my mother, to whom I had complained, that it was not his intention to 'convert' me, but it did feel like that at the time.

Over the following years my brother tried on several occasions to influence my views. I have a recollection of a family Christmas gathering where he tried to point out that no one could have 'come to the Lord' at a mission held in a Catholic university college as no Roman Catholics could be Christian. Even my parents disagreed with him. The argument ended after about two days when at a meal he stood up and said, 'Well, I am right, and you are all wrong' and left.

I now meet many people who have been hurt by and alienated

from their churches, friends, and families on religious matters. The hard-line views; the lack of compassion for, and inclusion, of LGBTQI+ people; the suppression of women and their capacity to be themselves and use all their gifts; discrimination against divorced people, and so on, has led to many losing their faith or struggling to find a place or way to worship God. Fortunately for me I have still been able to maintain family relationships, even if strained at times, and not been rejected. Nevertheless, I am accused by some to have lapsed or left the true path.

This is the story of my experience as I reflect on my journey of faith over a 60-year period. I was born into a conservative evangelical family with generations of Brethren and Strict Baptist Chapel people having gone before me. My mother's family were Plymouth Brethren with a mix of Presbyterian where no Brethren Congregation could be found. Later my grandfather, then a widower, marred an Anglican and started to attend Anglican churches, if they were evangelical enough. My father had been born in southern England and raised in the Strict and Particular Baptist Church. Although neither of my parents rebelled against their up-bringing, they did move away from the very conservative congregations during their university days. Both worshipped at St Gregory and St Martin Anglican Church, Wye while studying agriculture at Wye College (University of London). My parents maintained an adherence to a day of rest on Sunday where we were only able to attend Sunday School and church, read the Bible, and write letters to our grandparents. We were not allowed to play sport or go out and meet with friends. This began to change in my teens as my parents realised that we needed to be able to make our own choices as to where we would worship and socialise outside of the church community, unlike what had occurred in their childhoods.

I was born and raised in Armidale, NSW, where there are

many churches. My parents had settled on attending the Central Armidale Baptist Church, as they found the Anglican Church too 'High Church' for them. This later changed with a new Bishop and Dean, when my brothers began attending a youth group at the Cathedral and I started attending the University of New England Chapel. I had found worshipping at the Baptist Church had led to more questions than were being answered regarding my faith journey. Often the congregation split when a new minister arrived (usually from southern USA) and a disagreement would arise about a point of theology. My questioning and desire to grow my understanding of God's love came from one of the pastors who only stayed a few years, Jim Kime. Jim was much more liberal than his predecessors and provided an environment where younger people, such as me, could question and grow in our faith. Nevertheless, I still found the Baptist church stifling, and therefore explored other places to worship. My parents were happy for me to do this rather than stop attending anywhere, thus I found myself at the University Chapel.

One of the University chaplains was a very progressive evangelical called Kevin Giles, who was in the forefront of the debate on the role of women in the church and the push to ordain women as priests in Australia. I also admit that I enjoyed the Chapel because there were more interesting and intelligent young men there! It was through the Chapel that I met my husband, although we married five years later. I found a spiritual home here and began a journey from the judgement and damnation version of the Christian faith to a view that God had made us all equal, all valued and loved, and all in the image of God. I have come to understand that we have Christ within us and are called to be examples of Christ to others. I therefore no longer had to believe and do certain things to be 'saved' nor demonstrate my religious credentials to those in authority to be accepted.

This more incarnational view of the world was further developed as I grew older. My husband offered himself for ministry and we found ourselves at, a 'middle of the road' Anglican theological college in Canberra. The students and staff came from a variety of places, backgrounds, and theological perspectives. On the one hand the College was traditionally Anglican in its ethos and theology, yet on the other it was more liberal than conservative. It was a challenging yet enjoyable time as we both explored our faith and learnt about a range of theological viewpoints. While I had been baptised as an adult at my old Baptist Church I was later received into the Anglican Church while my husband was studying theology.

The confrontation with my brother came towards the end of our time at college. My brother was also studying for the ministry but at Moore College in Sydney. He had developed a much more theologically conservative faith that mirrored much of our parents' views and earlier family backgrounds. A major area of conflict was in the role of women in the church. My parents accepted women in leadership and preaching roles while my brother maintained a complete male headship view. I did stir both him and his friends at his ordination in St Andrew's Cathedral, Sydney by wearing a 'Priest women now' badge and was almost thrown out of the Cathedral. (The Diocese of Sydney took legal action against the Diocese of Canberra and Goulburn to stop the first ordination of women in 1992. As of 2023 it continues to refuse to ordain women as priests and only allows women to be ordained to the diaconate). This was decades before the current debates on homosexual bishops, same-sex relationships and marriage, abortion and women's choice, which are prevalent today.

Another aspect of my upbringing was the importance of mission. My parents supported several missionary societies financially, in prayer, and by attending summer schools and conventions. I can remember missionaries coming to stay in our home and describing what they were doing. Each year we attended CMS Summer School at Katoomba and I continued to do this through my university years. My parents also became missionaries in Indonesia with CMS after my father had retired from full time work. This strong interest in missionaries came from my mother's family. The Katoomba Convention, based on the English Keswick Convention, had been started in 1903 by my mother's grandparents, Ernest and Margaret Young, on the lawns of their summer residence 'Khandala' in Katoomba. For at least its first 50 years this convention provided the mixing ground for Plymouth Brethren, evangelical Anglicans from Sydney and Melbourne, Presbyterians, and other protestant denominations in Sydney. Initially, support for missions, prayer, and hearing the experiences of visiting missionaries was an integral part of the program. Some of the great missionaries, such as Hudson Taylor, attended and stayed with the family along with senior clergy from Sydney evangelical circles who came to speak and led Bible studies. The Convention later became dominated by the teachings, beliefs and practices of Sydney Anglican Evangelicalism and a place for formation of young people in this narrower form of Christianity.

One of my mother's aunts, Florence Young, had started the Queensland Kanaka Mission in Bundaberg, Queensland with Florence Buchanan. The 'Kanaka' were indentured and sometimes forced labour from the Pacific who came to Australia from the 1860s to work in the cane fields of Queensland and northern NSW. The term 'Kanaka' is now seen as derogatory and has been replaced by 'South Seas islanders'. Most were deported back to their home islands in the early 1900s after Australia adopted its White Australia Policy. Those who remained found it very hard to find work and were often subject to discrimination. This later became the South Seas Evangelical Mission in the Solomon Islands when many of the Islander labourers in the sugar industry were returned/deported by the Australian Government after the introduction of the 1901 White Australia policy. The mission had been started to provide schooling and a Sunday School to the Islander labourers and their families. This continued in Solomon Islands and included medical and dental care until the Second World War. The organisation is now known as the South Seas Evangelical Church and is the third largest Christian denomination in the Solomon Islands.

As an adult I have remained in the Anglican Communion, finding the more traditional service, choral music, and the changing liturgy of the Church year to be a solid base for my faith. This includes regular Lent and Advent studies produced by inspiring writers rather than weekly Bible studies. I have found that being part of a broad community is more important to me than being inside a safe but black and white judgemental congregation. Over the past 12 years we have lived and worked in Sydney where the Anglican diocese has become more hard-line theologically with one archbishop even saying, 'if you don't agree with my view on the blessing of same sex marriages you can leave' and people, especially the young or those with gay friends and family, have left in droves.

For me, Sydney Anglican Evangelicalism (among other ultra-conservative religious denominations) has provided a negative view of Christianity and has now become detrimental to the mission of the church both here in Australia and in other parts of the world. I understand it to be more interested in law than grace, which is reflected in an obsession with conservative social policies and reactionary politics.

With retirement and a move to the country I have found

a local ecumenical community of faith that worships in a little corrugated iron church. Here anyone can join and feel safe and welcome regardless of social standing, sexuality, race, or religion.

My brother and I have now found mutual ground that does not involve discussion of religion, politics or the church. Maintaining family relationships was more important, so we keep the relationship at a light and social level. He has now stopped trying to convert me back to being a 'Bible believing' (Sydney Anglican) Christian. Nevertheless, he does not seem to respect or accept my faith experience or position and there are still derogatory comments made about traditional worship and progressive theology; and he has continued to try and get my daughter to attend one of the 'approved' Sydney Anglican churches and young adult groups. Some of his beliefs have changed and mellowed in the last few years when he began working with indigenous Christians in inner Sydney, but he appears to remain hard-line on many matters such as the role of women in the church, believing that women can only minister to other women and children; that LGBT+ people aren't considered Christian and certainly cannot hold leadership roles in the church; and holding very conservative political views including supporting Donald Trump because he was considered politically 'pro-life' regardless of all his personal immorality and racism.

In the last six months of my father's life, I watched him become more fearful of death and questioning whether he had lived a godly enough life to be saved and receive eternal life. I found this sad as his life had been one of service and witness, always helping people in their own faith journey. He had returned to his fundamentalist roots. As each of his children and grandchildren came to visit, he would express his unease at their relationship with their 'Lord and Saviour', and no longer respected the decisions they had made regarding the Christian faith.

When I was challenged, I turned the conversation around and said I was content with the relationship with God that I had and the faith journey I was on. Dad backed off, but I think he still felt I had given up the faith example and beliefs he had provided to me in childhood.

I like to feel that I am living my life as an example of someone who has a personal faith with Jesus and an assurance of eternal life present in the here-and-now, which includes being a compassionate person using my gift of hospitality to make people feel welcome and included. This is a more incarnational view – Christ is in me, and I hope it shows. I strongly believe we gain an understanding of God, Christ, and the Holy Spirit from those around us (Christian and non-Christian); from the traditions of the church including using the lectionary to read all parts of the Bible, the sacraments and liturgy; using other methods of studying the bible such as Lectio Divina, rather than a perpetual exegesis of Romans; meditation, spiritual direction, and retreats. I also feel that what I was taught in my earlier years was just the milk of faith and not the solid food needed to function in the complex world as an adult witness. Humans don't know it all and there is a need to contemplate the mystery and encounter the Spirit in faith. For me the Christian faith is not just a matter of possessing obscure intellectual knowledge coupled with pious actions that are approved by church leaders.

A more recent challenge to my faith has come with the growing consciousness of the negative impact of colonialism and missionaries on the indigenous peoples of Australia and other parts of the world – a view that suggests that white culture (including Christianity) was better than whatever existed anywhere else previously. Fortunately, this is now being challenged. I have been immensely proud of my family's missionary endeavours, yet now

I search for the other side of the story as well. I have found other Christian based missionary organisations to support, which I feel are more Christ centred and take into consideration the needs and culture of others first. I now look for organisations that are ecumenical and not judgemental. Sadly, I have seen a few examples in my lifetime of conservative Christian organisations prioritising credal considerations above the basic needs of life. An example is the Hamlyn Foundation which established fistula hospitals for women in Ethiopia. A dispute arose within the Foundation about who could be partners with the work in the hospitals. The then CEO believed that the partners should all be Christian-based. The Australian fundraising arm agreed, and refused to send funds when the CEO was removed.

In my professional life as an archivist there has also been change. The profession has been challenged to arrange and describe archival material differently, decolonialise terms and make narratives more accessible, and provide access for alternative stories, historical views of events, people, and places, thereby allowing for alternative histories to be written.

I suppose the main thing that has caused me think that a less judgemental and inclusive faith journey has been right for me and reflects a more Christ-like way, has been seeing the damage to people and their faith caused by a very exclusive and judgemental stance taken by some in the Sydney Anglican Evangelical group. The Anglican communion is now losing its 'broad church' way and is being replaced by extremes of black and white narrowness on one side and a traditional church just trying to maintain a position yet not really addressing the issues of the world in which we live in on the other. Just adding modern music and adopting careless self-focused liturgy will not bring thinkers, young people, and women back to the Christian faith. There are so many people hurt, confused and just downright angry who are leaving the church, with some rejecting Christianity completely.

In Australia, a type of persecution of anyone with Christian views has been identified as people reject the socio-political stance of church institutions. There has also been a loss within the community of faith of a safe space for people to come and worship, question and learn, share their doubts and fears, serve others, and obtain challenging preaching so that we can go out and be an example of Christ to the world.

To understand God and Jesus in a personal way one must include the Spirit. The Trinity (or God in community) is a foundation of the Christian faith, yet this seems to be missing in some parts of the conservative church. Here hierarchy, conformity, and the exercise of power seem to overrule the communal life, exemplary behaviour, spirituality, and the traditions of the church. For my part, I understand that Christ taught us to be more respectful and loving of our neighbours rather than seeking to judge, disregard, or control them.

Iwerne to Yoga

Nicholas Harris

When Charles first asked me to write something for this book, I felt honoured to be invited, but also felt a little disheartened that my one and only contribution to a book on religion would be on the theme of apostasy, an offering which would include reference to my own experience. I felt sad because apostasy is usually seen in quite a negative light in terms of the church's history. It has been a term used to describe the departures of various people from 'the one true faith', these people themselves being 'in error'. A little later though, I sat thinking carefully about the word and its Greek roots 'apo' and 'histeemi'. These words literally mean 'away' and 'I stand' and I began to think that 'standing away' from a problem or a situation, at least for a while, can be very positive. I have a friend who is a carpenter who will often leave a difficult job for a time when he is not sure what to do. He makes himself a cup of tea, and when he comes back, he realises what the job requires. As an artist myself, I appreciate being in a large room so that I can step back from my easel and appraise my work. Seeing it from a distance, I can more easily get a sense of what is needed, whether that be more contrast or a new block of colour to bring things into (or indeed out of) balance, etc. I found myself wondering whether the same could be true of religion. I hope so, because I seem to have been someone who, on a number of occasions, stepped back from religion. Each time I have also returned with, I hope, a deeper and richer understanding. So now to the beginning of my 'Apostate's tale'.

My own early faith was Christian. I was at Stowe, an independent evangelical Christian-based school. It wasn't a bad place as boarding schools go. There was a fairly wide variety of activities and the first headmaster J. F. Roxburgh prided himself on a culture in which every 'Stoic' (the name given to someone who attended the school) could be an individual.

For all Stowe's qualities, it was a boarding school: children were separated from their parents. Inevitably, without parental nurture and care, pupils had to look after and parent each other as best we could. It worked surprisingly well, and we did our best in many ways. There were, however, acts of great cruelty carried out by some individuals, and that was where the absence of parental supervision was felt most strongly. There was bullying. For a time I was one of the bullies, and for a time I found my cruelty exciting. But I couldn't but notice the quiet misery of my victims.

At about the age of 15, most of us as a matter of routine signed up for 'Confirmation' classes. These classes were designed to introduce us more deeply to the Christian faith such that we could, should we wish, commit ourselves to this faith and be 'confirmed' in our decision by the local Bishop. The classes didn't seem any more or less interesting than any other school subjects felt to me at that time but then, after a number of weeks, we went on a 'Retreat' for two or three days.

There I had a transformative encounter with Jesus. I felt him to be a living presence. I returned to school with a feeling of extraordinary joy, determined from then on to be kind to the less popular boys. I did find I could do this and I believed and believe that Jesus, whom I considered and consider to be present to me in some mysterious way, helped me to do that. It was a great change in my life and I was so happy. I should also mention another part of the teaching on the Retreat: we heard that Jesus wanted his followers to follow a path of sexual purity. In this vein, Jesus didn't like people lingering on sexual thoughts or masturbating. This strangely resonated with a disquiet about the practice which I was already feeling, and I felt that renunciation was a small price to pay for my new friendship with this wonderful man.

I was as high as a kite for many weeks and persuaded the school chaplain to let me stand up and tell the school about my discovery during one of the week-day chapel services. I gave up my bullying and began to treat my former victims with kindness. My euphoria continued for a number of weeks. The only thing that spoiled it was my inability to stop dwelling on sexual thoughts. During the euphoric phase it was easy to comply with all this but as the euphoria subsided, so the thoughts grew and I wasn't clear what I could do about them. We were told by our mentor Christian advisors to ask Jesus to help us to overcome these thoughts, but for some reason unknown to me at the time, he didn't help. I became worried and distressed and remember one weekend (illegally) downing a bottle of cider and going to the school chapel to look at the painting of Jesus behind the altar. He seemed remarkably distant and uninterested in my plight. I wanted to have another go at speaking with the school and updating my peers on my journey some months down the line. This second talk would have included an account of my disappointment with Jesus for not helping me around sexual abstinence. My speech was vetted by an assistant chaplain who didn't seem to be happy with some of what I wanted to say and suggested I revise my proposed talk. I don't remember exactly what he said, but the gist of it seemed to be that instead of focusing on things such as Jesus' not helping me to control my sexuality, I was to be more upbeat, acknowledging that there were difficulties in the Christian life whilst affirming strongly that Jesus was an ever-present helper. I yielded and adjusted my talk but realise now that I had in effect been censored. This moment of censorship was to mark the beginning of a process of suppression in which I would find myself trapped for a number of years.

I attended the weekly 'Christian Forum' at the school, where Christians gathered, encouraged each other in our 'Christian Life' and listened to talks by visiting speakers. The informality and gentle hospitality of the meetings helped us and we would all leave feeling so much better in every way. The other body to which I was invited and with which I was to be involved for many years was the organisation which ran the now notorious summer camps at Iwerne Minster in Dorset – in a hired boarding school. I want to say that for many of us, the camps were occasions of great joy. In spite of their name, they were not held under canvas. There was much friendship, kindness and fun to be had. The rules about sex still applied but somehow in such an affectionate and joyful atmosphere, troublesome thoughts about sex dropped away. Each time I left, I felt exhilarated and vowed never to masturbate again. Such vows lasted at best a week and usually were broken within a day or two. I felt troubled by this and in retrospect I realise that, though I was with a group of extremely good and kind people, a number of us were placed in great difficulties by the very strict teachings about sex. I believe that many boys did find they could abstain from sexual practices and, in time, did find themselves settling into happy, lifelong, Christian marriages. Many of us, though, could not. This brought me great distress, which could only be alleviated by the joy of the camps and Christian meetings, but never ultimately resolved. I kept going to 'Camp' during my school years and continued attending during university. At university (I read classics at Cambridge) I became a 'senior camper' (the term given to those helping with the domestic chores at Iwerne during their University years). Then at some point I was invited by David Fletcher, the Iwerne camp leader, into the 'Officers' Room'. I was now part of the leadership of the Iwerne camps. I began to give talks there and visited the Christian groups at the various schools from which boys would attend Iwerne. During my time at university I felt a 'call' to the ordained ministry of the Church.

As a leader I was part of the praying and teaching body of leaders who would seek to help those boys who felt ready to 'open their lives' to Jesus. This part of officer life felt sincere as many boys did want to make that step. I do feel however, looking back, that we might have been too dogged in the help we offered. We used to say to a boy in our care: 'Have you opened the door of your life to Jesus or are you still thinking about it?' We were not directly pushing anyone into Christian commitment but the alternative ('are you still thinking about it?') was nonetheless directional. It might have been better to share our own beliefs and experiences but then also to ask the boys what their thoughts about life and spirituality were. We might then have supported them in their own growing spiritual understanding. By the same token it would have been better to hear about other philosophies of life, religious and non-religious, both at school and at Iwerne. Furthermore it feels to me now to have been a mistake to have been so directive towards people regarding sex and relationships.

There were some very lovely married couples involved with Iwerne and in my church back home. They seemed so wholesome and the young people who had come from 'Christian homes' often seemed integrated and relaxed. There is so much to be said for Christian marriage and the kind of committed family life that goes with it. But so few of us were in such a safe haven. We seethed with unfulfilled sexual longings. David Fletcher the camp leader, whom I found to be a lovely supportive father figure over a number of years, was also, however, very strict when it came to sex. He would tell us that sex was good but that it was like fire and should therefore be handled very carefully and kept strictly in the bounds of the 'fire grate' (marriage). If it was not kept there it could set fire to the whole house, he explained. In our student years, we were considered too young for relationships. These should wait until we were of marriageable age. In our teens and early twenties we should make the most of our single states to grow as Christians and evangelise our fellow students. This edict was not of course enforceable, and a few brave souls managed to defy the guidelines, but many others got caught up in this notion and thereby trapped in all sorts of internal contradictions.

Looking back at these 'Iwerne' thoughts about sex through my school, university and even ordination training, I feel a deep sadness for my 'younger self' and for other 'younger selves' who suffered so. Romance and sex are, after all, I now realise such a great gift to us in so many forms other than in a committed marriage.

I find, too, that I want to review all that happened in those days. I find myself appealing to Jesus and asking him if, in his compassion and kindness, he would really have wanted those of us who were troubled by the rules to be living in sexual torment, or whether he would have relaxed those rules for those of us who could not attain the lofty heights whereby we would wait, while all those teenage hormones raged, until the moment of lifelong marriage arrived. For myself I think it could have been lovely if relationships of all kinds had been supported and how beautiful it could have been if, as leaders, we were also exploring our romantic and sexual feelings. We could then have brought our stories and experiences to 'Camp' and, in the context of a supportive Christian group, we could then have learned together how to demonstrate kindness to ourselves and to 'the other' in all our surrendering to Love's spell.

None of this was possible though. Instead, for those of us without the ability to 'hold on', our sexual feelings would often be experienced in ways which brought misery to ourselves and even harm to others.

When I had finished my undergraduate degree, I spent a year in London helping out in a church and working in a Sainsbury's in Stepney. My close association with the Iwerne movement continued and I thoroughly enjoyed the friendships there but now a new odd thing happened. I had decided that I wanted, when I had finished my undergraduate degree and this work experience year in London, to train for the ordained ministry at Wycliffe Hall in Oxford. I fancied a change from Cambridge, but Mark Ruston, the vicar of the Round Church, and a leading figure in Iwerne, who had been kind to me in many ways and to whom I had become very close, had other thoughts. He wanted me to return to Cambridge to become the Iwerne lead student officer there and so, rather than encouraging my desire to go to Oxford, he adopted the tactic devised and often used by Eric Nash, the founder of the Iwerne camps. He made me 'feel a cad'. Because of this I decided to stay in Cambridge and to train at Ridley Hall whilst also taking a theology degree at the University. It was round about this time that I had another shock from the Iwerne movement . At least one person in the organisation told me that studying theology was a waste of time and that I should use my time at Ridley to evangelise students instead. Others tut-tutted about the 'woolly liberals' and 'universalists' at the Divinity faculty.

This harmful and unkind attitude can be traced back to Nash who used to stamp out any theological debate in the 'Officers' Room', saying sharply: 'We don't discuss theology in this room'.

Although Nash was great fun and had the kind of face and manner that made you want to laugh joyfully, he was fiercely anti-intellectual and controlling in the area of theology, which was to the detriment of Iwerne: there were so many highly intelligent people there, many of whom did nevertheless take theological study seriously. I entered theological study with alacrity and delight, combining my ordination training with a second degree in the University Divinity faculty.

Initially, as I studied, I felt my evangelical roots being bolstered by so much valuable information. But then came the challenges. In my New Testament studies, I came to understand the difficult but fascinating task of finding 'the gospel behind the gospels', that is to say, what Jesus actually said and did as against what the evangelists said he said and did. I saw for the first time how strangely different Jesus was from us. I read Albert Schweizer's *Quest for the Historical Jesus* and was amazed at his courage after he had established his findings about the 'eschatological apocalyptic prophet' named Jesus. In terms of systematic theology, I was very fortunate to be able to study with Rowan Williams, at that time a young man and a deeply compelling and attractive figure in the Divinity Faculty. He helped me understand and interpret texts from pseudo-Dionysius the Areopagite, Aquinas and Schleiermacher. Even more valuable than this was his kindness and his gift of time, which he gave extravagantly. I attended the lectures of Don Cupitt as Cupitt explained the gradual unwinding of 'Realism' in theology, and looked to the socio-linguistic functions of religion. I was touched and able to re-assess my thinking in the safe space provided by the thoughtful compassion of Rowan Williams, and it was the intellectual courage of Don Cupitt which struck me to the core. I had always thought that Christian faith must prioritise both truth and love and, although I had found much love and kindness in my

Iwerne circles, I felt I had never met people of such transparent intelligence and integrity as these two people. I felt that I was moving quite rapidly away from my evangelical roots, which was awkward given that I was Iwerne lead officer at Cambridge.

I had a chance to do a student swap for a month with someone from Westcott House, the other Anglican theological college in Cambridge. I told Mark Ruston what I was doing, and he didn't seem completely comfortable, perhaps because Westcott was more liberal in its approach to theology and Christian life. Nevertheless I went, and loved my time there. It was such a relief to be away from the solemn faces and figures of the great Reformers, one on each window in the chapel in Ridley. Instead, I found myself in the empty white space of Westcott chapel, with its one beautiful icon of the Mother and Child. It was like being in a womb where I was not being 'steered' or 'preached at' but rather, held and loved. There were all sorts of fascinating people at Westcott House, including the Principal, Rupert Hoare, whose doctoral thesis had been a study of the relationship between Rudolph Bultmann (one of the most profound New Testament scholars of the twentieth century) and psychoanalysis.

Being at Westcott House felt so refreshingly honest and exploratory. People there were embracing their intellectual journey and by and large seemed less dissociated and more in touch with their feelings. I was still fond of my evangelical friends, but I could not help but find them somewhat afraid of all the people and thinking was now discovering. I also became more profoundly aware of the deep frustrations in myself which had built up over the years. I have described the experience of sexual repression. To this I would now add the resistance I had felt in some parts of the Iwerne community against my making a serious study of theology. In these two areas I began to feel I had been first castrated and then secondly decapitated (or at any rate

I had narrowly escaped such an injury to my brain). These are strong words, but my feelings were by now running high. There was a third feeling: a sense of evisceration. I say this because my feelings in all their complexity just had not been taken sufficiently seriously by my mentors during my Iwerne days. Feelings were acknowledged, but the thought was that we should not dwell on them, particularly if they were sad or anxious. Rather we should look to Jesus, giving thanks to him for his death on the cross for our sins. Then our troubled feelings would come right. I understood this to a degree, but it didn't seem to go nearly close enough to what I was wanting. And thus it was, in the light of what I felt to be this triple bodily wounding, that I sat down and wrote a short story called *The Story of a Machine; Its Making and Destruction*, in which I took and re-wrote a familiar evangelical wisdom parable. In this parable, the Christian disciple 'Faith' is on a tightrope looking at Jesus who is on the rope ahead of him. Coming up in the rear is 'Feelings' who is forever trying to unsettle 'Faith' and make him look back. If Faith looks back, he will stop looking at Jesus and may then fall off the rope. But if he keeps looking at Jesus, Faith will be okay. In my version, though, the spotlight was on Feelings, who is looking ahead at Faith and sees an emaciated, castrated, decapitated and eviscerated figure. Feelings calls out, telling Faith what he sees. Faith, though, is so incapacitated that he can no longer even hear what Feelings is telling him, until in one last desperate attempt to get through, Feelings reaches out a hand towards Faith, thereby also dislodging him from the rope. Faith, by this time bereft of his essential body parts, has become like a machine, and as he hits the ground he explodes into a thousand mechanical pieces.

One evening, late at night, I put a copy through Mark Ruston's door. Mark was of course deeply upset and told me I had got the wrong end of the stick. He invited me to stay with him for a few days so that we could hammer things out. But I was by now running in the other direction. I stayed on as lead officer of the Cambridge Iwerne group for a few weeks, thinking perhaps I could change things for the better. At one point I had a conversation with a senior Iwerne officer who understood theology, thinking I could find some support from him. I asked him how he managed to survive at Iwerne knowing what he knew, and I realised that my question had put him on the defensive as I was greeted with a rather stony face. Nevertheless, I pressed on and told him I thought I would stay on as Lead student officer as I felt I would be able to change things for the better. To this notion, my fellow-officer replied, 'Are you God?' Almost forty years later, I still don't really understand the purport of his question but it was enough to deflate me. Shortly afterwards I resigned my place as Lead student officer, deciding that I needed to carve out a different future for myself.

This departure from Iwerne was perhaps my first act of apostasy and, unfortunately it was more of a flight than a 'standing back with a view to appraise'. I am conscious too in looking back that these words represent a rather harsh critique of Iwerne. I suppose breakups between mentors and their protégées are often violent. I wouldn't though in all this want to underestimate all that I gained from Iwerne: the beginnings of my journey in faith, the fun and the laughter and the kindness and support the community there offered. There was the sexual repression and what was in my opinion, a certain self-imposed ceiling on intellectual and emotional intelligence, but for all this, I hold these people in my heart and shall always be grateful to them.

Thinking a bit more about the notion of apostasy: although I had stood back from Iwerne, I had not stood away from the Christian faith, at least as I had begun to understand it. I appreciate though that in what follows, some will consider me at this point to be way beyond its boundaries. By the time that I was ordained, I was already, given my forays into philosophical theology, agnostic about the 'existence' of God, but I stayed with religion and the Church because I felt they had an important role to play in society. Building on Cupitt, I came to see Christian worship as best understood in terms of 'performative' ritual and language and in my first church on Walney Island in Barrow-in-Furness in Cumbria (a church in the liberal catholic tradition), I wanted to explore what that might mean. I was still deeply moved by the person of Jesus and his kindness and compassion. I felt this was a beautiful story to stand in the middle of a community, and indeed few communities exemplified and 'mirrored back' better the values of Jesus than the lovely people of Walney. I was also fascinated watching how people behaved in groups, how buildings affected people, and how meeting for no reason other than to reflect on a story affected people. The spacious scale of a church building, the shared presence of a community, and sacred words spoken slowly from a place of deep breath, transformed us each Sunday as we met. I was, as I have already said, by now quite agnostic as to whether the Jesus story was describing an actual God or gods. I think, like Cupitt and the early Wittgenstein on whom he had built much of his thinking, my thought was that 'that of which we cannot speak, we should be silent'. But then too in terms of the later Wittgenstein, I was understanding and inhabiting the 'language game' of faith and witnessing how religious language could affect, express and enhance a community. I didn't share these kinds of thoughts with the congregation or even with Philip Ward, the vicar, who was a learned man. My relationship with Jesus still stood firm. I was comforted too in this by the thought that Jesus was, according to my reading of the gospels, more interested in how people believed, than in what they believed.

My three years on Walney Island were among the happiest in my life. There was no anxiety about converting people, and yet people brought their children in large numbers to be baptised and thereby initiated into the church. Somehow the church was part of the community as much as the local shop, the pub and the laundrette. Everyone I met recognised it as having a part to play on the island and people would come joyfully and worship joyfully. Those who had no religious belief still loved the church and were glad when their children attended the Church youth club.

Being on Walney confirmed in me a growing hunch that the world was not made up of the saved and the damned.

I was still immensely curious to know what was happening in the world of work. Were secular work places the seat of 'evil principalities and powers', or just groups of people like the communities of Walney Island – good people doing their best to earn a daily crust? Unable to find the answer to this question in Barrow-in-Furness, I applied for a job as an industrial chaplain with the South London Industrial Mission. I met people in a huge variety of jobs.

My years as an industrial chaplain provided me too with the answers to questions I had long been asking. Did the world need to be saved? And was I an essential agent in that salvific process? I was asking these questions because a deeper part of me wanted to be an artist rather than a priest. Those years in south London left me feeling that the world could do its own thing while I could do mine. I resigned from full-time church ministry, moved to Sussex, and taught myself to paint. I did continue in part time ministry and explored the relationship between Faith and the Arts.

As I did, a lifetime of muddled and repressed sexual feeling exploded, and I also discovered God as not just a word in a societal 'language game' but as something or someone with agency in the world – someone who loved me profoundly.

I discovered that I could paint. It gave me confidence that I could do something other than passively listen – which I saw as one of the major parts of the work of a priest.

I fell in love, but my romantic inexperience meant that I couldn't cope. I torpedoed a precious relationship, telling the woman to fuck off. She did, deeply hurt. I had a nervous breakdown in which I could not sleep. For months I could scarcely hold down any food. I compulsively brushed my teeth all through the day as if to wash my mouth out. I couldn't be on my own without falling into a panic attack. Often I couldn't breathe. I survived – but only just – with the help of some friends who took me into their home.

It was a terrible but wonderful time. Being so incapacitated for many months, I was able to see the world in a new way. I experienced how much help and love there was 'out there'. Strange things happened – wonderful synchronicities – which persuaded me that I was being looked after by 'someone' or 'someones' not directly perceptible in the physical world. It was an extraordinary conclusion to reach: it went against all my philosophical thinking. It made no sense, but that was my experience.

I went on to explore my renewed faith more deeply. Although of course I had my Christian roots, I was now living in a world of artists, many of whom explored their faith through the practice of yoga.

I again fell in love. This too was to be another problematic love for me, for the object of my love was a married woman. My priestly training got the better of me. I just could not forget my having wrapped my stole around so many young couples' clasped hands and then saying, 'What God has joined together, let not man put asunder'. I had not at this stage looked beyond the surface meaning of Jesus' words about marriage; nor had I considered here the wider context of his teachings. I censured myself fiercely and pushed the woman away. She got divorced and returned to me. Deciding I was probably the cause of her marriage breakdown, I pushed her away again. This led me to a second breakdown. It took five more years to recover fully.

It became clear that my yoga friends thought that I had been very wrong to push the woman away. I found this very distressing. It seemed to me that they no longer respected me. I looked again at the theology and ethics of divorce, and concluded that their censure was right.

This marked the beginning of my current apostasy – my current standing back from Christianity. In terms of the analogy of standing back from the easel, this standing back has lasted for years, not minutes or hours. Because I hadn't at this time sifted Jesus' words about marriage and divorce more deeply, I blamed him for the predicament in which I had got myself. I began too to feel other grievances towards him – in particular what began to feel to me like his extreme teachings in which his followers were to give up their lives, their possessions and all that they had, in order to follow him. What place could there still be for the practice of one's own life, the nurture of one's family and the honing and shaping of one's identity If one were only ever abandoning everything in order to follow him?. How could one look after oneself in the most basic of senses? I had always found this teaching difficult. Looking back over my life, I could see that at times I have thought too much about other people. I hadn't kept proper boundaries for myself and as a result people had taken advantage of me.

I began to teach yoga, and discovered through Eastern religion and philosophy what seemed to me to be a much kinder and gentler approach to spirituality. Gone were the ideas of the inherent wickedness of people and their need for salvation by some external force or being. Rather we were good, our bodies were whole and, by exploring them more deeply, we could deepen our own wholeness. As I studied Buddhist meditation, I discovered a great sense of restraint around metaphysical speculation. In Buddhism I discovered the 'Middle Way' in which one is enjoined neither to be too bad on the one hand nor too virtuous on the other. I was fascinated by the stories of how the Buddha attempted all sorts of extreme ascetic practices, including eventually almost starving himself to death. In one, the Buddha on the brink of starvation brought about by excessive fasting, was found under a tree by a group of children playing. They alerted their parents, who brought the Buddha back to their village where they fed him and brought him back to health. As he recuperated, the (wise) children visited and asked him why he had almost starved himself to death. It is a stern warning against life-denying extremism.

In terms of how all this relates to prayer and spirituality, what I have learned from Eastern spirituality could perhaps best be summarised in a Buddhist prayer/meditation – the Metta Bhavana. According to this prayer, you first bring your awareness to yourself, your body and your mind and feelings. You then bring your awareness to your close family and friends. After that you bring your awareness to those whom you know less well – perhaps people in your wider community of associates. Then you reflect on your village or town before finally bringing awareness to your country and to the rest of the world. I use the Metta Bhavana as a loose structure and often spend a lot of time on the first stages of the prayer before going onto the next. Often I never get past the first stage.

The Dalai Lama once said that he was very happy for people

of other faiths and spiritual traditions to visit and explore Buddhism, but that he hoped they would then be able to return to their own faiths. That's a lovely sentiment but it's surprisingly hard to achieve. The reality is that after an exploration of other traditions you are no longer the same person you once were, and what was once settled and normal for you can now look very odd in the light of your new and recent experiences. You can also feel fairly prickly towards your original religion for what you perceive to be its shortcomings – some of which it has taken a journey outside that religion to see. My journey into eastern spiritual practices had been a big 'stepping back' from Christianity, but could I, as the Dalai Lama suggested and hoped, go back? Could my stepping back be not a final flight but rather a 'stepping away' in order to return? And could I bring with me some of the wisdom I had garnered from 'the East'? Returning to my idea of apostasy as being like stepping back from a painting in order to see where new colour and shape might be needed, could I return to Christianity in that mode? Could I bring to Christianity the new colours and shapes I had discovered? Could I share my discoveries and have some constructive comments to make which might serve to enrich the Christian world? I had to ask too whether Christianity itself would want me on those terms? Would it entertain my suggestions? These are important questions because there was a chance that, with my newfound perspectives, I could create some upset too.

Until now I haven't really been discussing these matters a great deal with Christian people. But I have though been having conversations with the two people at the historic heart of Christianity – Jesus and St Paul.

I have put the following questions to Jesus: 'Granted that your high ethical standards are indeed the ideal for human life, will you please nevertheless allow your followers to bring to the table their own wisdom and methods for achieving them? Will you allow us to go at our own pace? Will you allow me please to bring to your 'Sermon on the Mount' my 'Metta bhavana'? Will you allow me and others on some days to keep back our cloaks for ourselves when we need simply to keep warm? Will you, above all, still love us even if we *never* get to where you are asking us to go?

The conversation continues.

I am not now agnostic. I believe in a personal God or gods because I have experienced a personal God (or gods) and this God is closer to me than my own breath. I love the intimacy with which Jesus connected to his God, calling him Abba Father — that is, 'Daddy'. As a teenager he opened that possibility to me and at times, when I am not so busy and preoccupied or worried but can just sit back and remember that God is right next to and in front of me, life again becomes a thing of beauty and wonder.

And St Paul? He indicates that to be Christian is to have died with Christ, and risen with Him. But do we lose too much by the type of death Paul seems to prescribe? Are our human lives and loves so irredeemably corrupt that death is necessary? Again, the conversation continues.

It's time for me to stop this piece of autobiography. I do realise in that I have a real nerve to think that I can leave the Church for twenty years and then come back and tell it what would make it easier for me to be part of things again! I am, I know, behaving very unlike the Prodigal who returned in sackcloth and ashes. And truly I don't expect this huge and venerable institution to turn on a sixpence on my account. I appreciate too, given some of my revelations and points of view that the Church may not want me anyway. I realise that other people's experiences of life (and perhaps too their temperaments) will have in good faith brought them to conclusions diametrically opposed to mine. And I do wish them well in all that they think and do. I am, meanwhile, grateful for this opportunity to share my thoughts on apostasy. It has certainly helped me make my peace with Jesus after many frosty years.

Secret Apostasy: A journey to freedom

Rosie Harper

At the core of my Christian formation was Good Friday. It was crucial in socialising me in church culture and it had a vice like grip on my theology.

In my home church we didn't really have a concept of Lent, but we might as well have done. As I think back I can almost hear the sound of heavy resonant booted steps as Good Friday approached.

There was a fun side. I joined the women of the church in a sandwich-making marathon. They were kind and gentle people who enjoyed teaching me how to make these weird little delicacies. We never had sandwiches at home – indeed I only ever ate white bread at church. There were other party food temptations: sausage rolls, fairy cakes, mini trifles. Of course the underlying given was that this was women's work. In church the wives cleaned and cooked and did all the clearing up afterwards. Some strong men might move a chair or a table. How very gracious of them.

But then came the terror. The Good Friday service was hard core. The idea was to look the story full in the face. To understand the depth of the suffering and in doing so grasp the seriousness of our sin and the cost of our forgiveness. The preacher did this very well. His story telling was superb. Every hammer blow tearing through flesh, every drowning breath, every shift from the pain of the limbs to the burn of the lungs was painted in gothic detail. I was drawn and repulsed in equal measure. The final twist was that this gifted preacher man was my father!

The seeds of cognitive dissonance were sown on those Fridays. The man I loved as my dad, who was a gentle and creative poet and artist, was telling me that my Heavenly Father was so appalled by me, even when I didn't think I was doing anything wrong, that he required this gross and extreme sacrifice to appease his anger. Because God loved me I didn't have to hang on the cross. He'd get his own son to do that.

Many years later, as a parish priest, it was my duty to lead people through Lent. This was by far the toughest part of my job. The introspection and self-denial felt like an extended experience of those early Good Fridays. In an imaginary conversation with my therapist I might even explore a weird sado-masochistic vibe. The form of conservative evangelicalism that I grew up in certainly had a disturbing elision of love and violence. From my present perspective I think this is why it seems perfectly okay for people to be unspeakably cruel to, for example, gay Christians, while genuinely thinking they are acting in love.

I guess I did all the things that children do when they grow up in a tight knit community. The community held me firmly within its theology. I was pretty anxious about being disobedient. I really hated the Scripture Union daily reading notes. Even then they seemed like holy Patience Strong, but I still felt guilty if I missed a day. Thus the habit of a sort of double life was born. I behaved one way and was a poster girl for a good Christian teenager, but in my imagination I was following a different script. At that young age I still felt that I was probably sinful and errant, and in the end I'd get chucked in the backslider dustbin. I read voraciously and was very excited by Tolstoy and Dostoyevsky. All the normal teenage desires were there of course, but it was impossible to act on them. There were some Christian boys in the youth group, but frankly they were idiots. I hugely regret not having lots of sex in those days like most of my friends at school and university. I now see the theology which said that you could only have a relationship with another Christian, and of course absolutely no sex before marriage, as a form of abuse. I know this sounds extreme, but there was a brittle Ice Queen side to my personality in those days which was a result of this abnormal environment.

At the time I didn't notice how I was mirroring my mother's life. She grew up in Zürich in a very tight Brethren church. She loved her parents and was totally unable to rebel in an overt way, but she developed a double life too. She lied about going to church in the evening after work and went to concerts instead. She was outwardly compliant but inwardly developed a different world view. She couldn't sustain it and left the country to escape rather than kick over the traces at home.

Except she didn't really escape! She ended up at London Bible College, met my dad and became a vicar's wife. The double life continued, just in another country.

Just like her I thought that leaving the home environment would set me free. I went to university and bravely refused invitations to the Christian Union. They talked and sang about Jesus as if he were their little imaginary friend and I certainly wasn't up for that!

I couldn't manage Sundays without any church at all, so I went to the local Anglican church. They were nice people there, the words were cosy and undemanding and the music was amazing. The organist was my professor of music and it was worth the twenty-minute walk just to hear him play every week.

It turned out, however, that, like my mother, I wasn't as free as I'd supposed.

I fell in love with a recent convert. To support him I went along to the Metropolitan Tabernacle, the home of the iconic reformed Baptist preacher Charles Haddon Spurgeon, and was plunged straight back into the arms of a judgemental angry God.

How did I endure those forty-five-minute sermons? Arrogant exegesis! But endure them I did.

Even though I was a good girl they eventually spat me out. By then I was a postgraduate opera student at the Royal Academy of Music and I was summoned in to Peter Masters' study (he was and I believe still is the minister). He made it clear that a real Christian had no business being involved with the theatre. We left.

Fondly imagining that it was a leap for freedom we began attending All Souls Langham Place. The music was just wonderful. I played the violin and sang solos. Noel Tredinnick the Music Director actually saw me as a real person with skills and gifts to contribute. Because of the music it didn't matter that I was a mere woman. Every church needs a good soprano!

The preaching was another matter. My dad went to the interminable series by Martyn Lloyd-Jones on the book of Romans at Westminster Chapel and witnessed the famous bust up between him and John Stott in 1966. That row is still going on. Although few in the 1960s actually heeded Lloyd-Jones and left the Church of England, most evangelicals thought that their allegiance to their tribe trumped their allegiance to their denomination. Plus ça change. Today, as we inch agonisingly towards better inclusion of LGBT people, lay and clergy, most conservative evangelicals won't actually leave but will make it clear that the bonds which bind them together are stronger and more important than their love for or loyalty to the Church of England.

In another strange mirroring experience, I ploughed through John Stott's Christian Counter-Culture series feeling just as manipulated as my dad felt at Westminster Chapel. At last I was beginning to make sense of the dissonance. In his rather charming urbane way Stott was telling me how God wanted me to live my life. As the penny dropped I began to feel angry. Here with an easy public school demeanour, was the same oppression of minorities (not that women are a minority of course) and that same rapacious hunger for power that misogyny demands around the world.

My husband went off to Wycliffe Hall but I stayed back and worked. I knew I'd suffocate at Wycliffe. In order to support him as a better vicar's wife I did a three-year pastoral counselling course with the Westminster Foundation and, as part of the therapeutic work, began to explore why I continued to occupy a space in the church I didn't believe in.

I recognised how many times I whispered to myself: 'Ah! If only you knew what I really think!' I also noticed how much spit and venom was involved in denouncing false teaching. Someone once told me that we become like the God we adore. There are folk out there who adore a very unpleasant God.

Being a vicar's wife turned out to be okay. Although still basically in the evangelical world the detail of parish life and family life was creative and life-affirming. No one cared what I believed, and that suited me. We looked out for one another in the parish. There was a lot of laughter, and especially through engagement with the local school there were ways of articulating a more generous faith. It felt fine sometimes to say: 'I'm not sure I quite see it like that.' I could recognise that little flicker across the face and knew they were thinking I was slipping, but it wasn't painful.

So yes, I was faking it. Conformity on the outside, but a secret traitor.

Full exposure came on 11 November 1992. Various folk in the parish and Diocese had given me nudges. Surely I'd make a good Deacon. Bah! I had watched too many women being treated as daddy's little helper. But when the vote for the ordination of women went through I was confounded. I won't super-spiritualise it, but I really felt I'd have a lot to offer. The Bishop lived down the road and I went a-knocking the very next day. In the rather charming way of the day I had a few chats with someone — I'm sorry to say I can't remember who — about art and music and travel. Possibly a little theology too — but thankfully I wasn't called upon to produce penal substitutionary atonement from my back pocket.

Then of course I had to fess up to my tribe. The local clergy for a start. I used to do morning prayer with Father Diamond in Deptford. He was a local hero and more Catholic than the Pope. He enjoyed teaching me his language. We got on really well. He died suddenly in August 1992 and I carried on going to morning prayer. I will never forget telling that group I was beginning training for ordination. For the first time my apostasy was not due to my false beliefs. I don't think they were that bothered about what I believed. The problem was simply that I was me. A woman. Game over. They didn't tell me what it said in the Bible; they didn't want to teach me a better way. They'd as soon ordain a penguin. It was simply impossible.

The evangelicals of course said they'd pray for me. I think they felt some sort of worm had got into my soul. Out came the Bible verses, the call to be faithful, the warning about following the secular world. It was all delivered with a sort of kindly sadness. The message was that they loved me but they knew that God would not want them to accept my calling. This became a common theme. The theology of violent love that I first glimpsed in my childhood allowed people to say and do all sorts of otherwise unacceptable things in the name of God. I grew to see this as spiritual infantilism. It was an inability to take moral responsibility for your actions, and an outsourcing of that responsibility to God. Hence the House of Bishops felt entitled to hound gay married clergy out of their jobs and homes in the name of unity.

The interesting thing about being a secret apostate is that when the game is up and it's no longer secret, the work, spiritually and emotionally has already been done. Once I stopped pretending to be one of the tribe things got so much better. My training was okay. I'm sure they thought I was a pain. I asked awkward questions and pushed at the boundaries in a way I should have done years before. I read all sorts of liberating books, discovered feminist theology and then absolutely delighted in taking a Philosophy MA.

I was beguiled by the space I found within the C of E to be myself. I rather fell in love with the local. By then my husband was Rector of a fabulous parish in Buckinghamshire and I became his curate. We were very different in the way we worked and in what we believed, but it was the sort of parish where there was space for that breadth, and I felt that I was flourishing. The imperfections seemed fixable (yes, I know: naïve or what?) and so I got stuck into Deanery and Diocese and eventually General Synod.

For a short time I honestly believed that the C of E was somewhere I could be myself and, much more than that, somewhere where others could be themselves too.

It didn't take long for reality to kick in. At a job interview, after I'd given my answer, a retired Bishop turned to his colleague and memorably said: 'She's brighter than she looks.' Good grief!

At another encounter with senior appointments I was told that the C of E needed people like me who asked the difficult questions and addressed the various elephants in its rooms. What they meant, but of course didn't say out loud was 'but not in senior roles'.

As time went by it became clear that although there were women priests in many roles, the theology was still rooted in an all-male world view – in a vision of a heroic Christian leader who had power and soft violence in his armoury. One pivotal experience was listening to a horrific account of a clergyman abusing his wife. She told her story and her parting shot was: 'It's the theology that did it.' There was that angry, controlling God right back in the room.

That same theology underpinned so much of the terrible treatment of LGBT+ people within the church. People have been driven to suicide or the brink of suicide basically because they are taught that the essence of who they are is unacceptable to God. The very people who have a strong and immutable understanding of a Just God have a very weak understanding of repentance. The recent Living in Love and Faith process will no doubt result in many apologies, but the church will surely prove unable to turn away from its abusive behaviour and make words about equality a lived reality.

Apologies abound in the world of safeguarding too. I now know many people who carry wounds too deep to bear. Not only has the church provided the careless environment in which horrors took place while others averted their eyes, but it has proved to be institutionally deaf to the demands for serious reform and redress. Yes, we now have training. The church has always done training and now we have a sort of Alpha Course for Safeguarding. But do we have mandatory reporting, or independent scrutiny, or benchmarking or a functioning redress scheme? We do not. Do survivors or those falsely accused feel that the church has treated them well? They do not.

A National Inquiry, IICSA, was needed to hold the church to account. It should be the other way round: the church could and should be a moral resource for the nation

It would be handy to separate these fault lines in the church from theology and see them as some sort of institutional disease. I'm not sure that is sufficient.

I have stepped back from involvement in the national Church. In the end what made me lose hope that I could be an agent for change and reform, even in a tiny way, was how the church was controlled from behind the scenes.

In a book on safeguarding in the CofE written with the Bishop of Buckingham, we said: 'The mark of a healthy and authentically Christian community is not large numbers, inspiring worship, or dogmatic theology, but the way in which power is exercised within it.'

The source of that power and the desire to exert it is belief in a controlling God. The clergy wife who was a survivor of serious domestic abuse was right: 'It's the theology that did it.'

Conclusion

Martyn Percy and Charles Foster

Our case studies have offered us some rare first-hand accounts of the trauma, trials and tribulations of moving from one faith – or one iteration of a faith – to another. To the traveller, the journey of faith may seem like an escape. Or a homecoming. Or a necessary separation and divorce from an abusive relationship to a new situation in which the primary benefits are safety and security. The common denominator is conversion: the abandonment of one's original faith community and its beliefs and practices, and the embracing of beliefs, practices and relationships in a different type of fellowship.

As editors, we have been puzzled, intrigued and alarmed by the multifaceted ways in which apostasy persists in the twenty-first century. We observe that for many of the faith communities featured in our case studies, members find it far easier to relate to individuals who lose all faith in God than those who adopt different-but-related beliefs. We also observe that the *scale* of conversion and change does not correlate well with the magnitude of the response from the community left behind. A move to Eastern Orthodoxy from conservative evangelicalism might be more psychologically (and perhaps more theologically) palatable to conservative evangelicals than one from conservative evangelicalisms to charismatic evangelicals. Perhaps we should not be surprised. We tend to be kinder to strangers than to our neighbours.

The term 'conversion' is part of our everyday language. It simply means 'to turn' – one currency into another, electricity into light or heat, or from one utility provider to another. In the field of faith a convert is someone who has turned away from something (or nothing) and embraced a faith. The 'new' faith need not in fact be new, for conversion can constitute some form of 're-turning'. Conversion, in this context, usually denotes a seismic change of an individual or a community. Some scholars consider that there are three distinct elements to conversion: tradition, transformation and transcendence. We might argue about how distinct these elements are, but at least they provide a useful framework on which to hang thoughts about the conversion process.

'Tradition' refers to the contextual aspects of both the convert and the relevant religious group. It encompasses such aspects of the conversion process as relationships with groups, members and non-group members, the previous life of the convert, institutional conduct, symbols, rituals and so on, as well as ideological and cultural aspects of religious tradition (for instance the ways in which culture impacts on conversion, and vice versa).

'Transformation' refers to the personal aspects of change in thoughts, beliefs, and actions through a study of experience, selfhood and consciousness. This process may be viewed through various interpretative lenses. William James, for instance, in *The Varieties of Religious Experience*, suggests that anguish, conflict or guilt may predispose individuals towards conversion.

'Transcendence' refers to encounters with the sacred, which for many religions is the goal of conversion. Theologically, the perceived relationship with the divine which is inherent in religious experience is central to an analysis of conversion.

According to Lewis Rambo, these three dimensions to conversion – tradition, transformation and transcendence – lead to at least five different types of conversion: 'Tradition transition', 'Institutional transition', 'Affiliation', 'Intensification' and 'Apostasy'. These are overlapping categories. Many of the case studies in this book exhibit more than one of the dimensions. It is important to note, too, that the category or categories into which a particular faith journey fits may depend on who is asked to comment. One traveller's Institutional Transition may be another's apostasy.

1. *Tradition transition* refers to conversion from one major or traditional religion to another. This may occur on a population level through political change, mass evangelisation, economic pressure or simple exposure to a different culture – for instance the mass conversions to Christianity following European colonialisation in the eighteenth, nineteenth and twentieth centuries.

    In this book, Nicholas Harris is perhaps an example – though an equivocal example. His world view has been crucially informed by his contact with Buddhism, and perhaps would not have been so informed – or informed in the same way – had he not found the conservative Christianity of his younger years (if it was indeed Christianity at all) unable to address (or even to acknowledge) the questions he came to see as central to the human condition. Yet he characterises his journey as a process of stepping back – a process that enables a better view. The better view of Christianity that he now has, has, it seems, begun to re-enchant Christianity for him.

He has an active conversation with Jesus and Paul. Harris finds himself 'appealing to Jesus' and asking him if he really wanted the church to be the way that conservative Christianity insisted it should be. Harris's tale is one of wrestling with God; not letting go until his questions are answered. And that, we recall, is how God wants it to be. Jacob was blessed and given that resonant name, 'Israel', precisely because that's what he did. Perhaps Harris, far from being an apostate, is one of the most orthodox and faithful Christians in these pages.

Anthony Bash grew up as a secular Jew before moving to Christianity, having become convinced of the historicity of the resurrection of Jesus. The move was costly and painful for him and his family. It was seen as a sell-out to Christianity — one of the ancient enemies of Judaism. Bash himself, however, seems to have been *theologically* a fairly blank slate.

2. *Institutional transition* involves changing allegiance from one sub-group within a major religion to another — for example switching between denominations of Christianity either for convenience of location or because of religious experience or a shift in belief.

There are many examples of this in this book: Dan Warnke moved from the Vineyard to High Anglicanism; Richard Baxter from Roman Catholicism to conservative evangelicalism — a move he sees as a change from unbelief to Christianity; Fife from non-conformism to charismatic evangelicalism and then to a more expansive form of Anglicanism; Charles Foster, from the Iwerne movement, to charismatic Anglicanism, and finding later a sustaining home in Eastern Orthodoxy; Thomas Bohache from Roman Catholicism to a type of Christianity which accommodated his convictions about his own identity and personhood and his belief that 'religion, at its very heart, calls us to wholeness and personal authenticity'; Anthony Bash from secular Judaism to evangelical Christianity and then, via the questions spawned by his study of academic theology, to a more liberal Protestantism; Ian Markham from the Exclusive Brethren to Anglicanism; Rosemary Sempell from conservative evangelicalism to liberal Christianity; Nicholas Harris from conservative evangelicalism to High Anglicanism; and Rosie Harper, who moved through various evangelical denominations before concluding that she was a 'secret apostate' (at least in relation to the toxic brands of Christianity she had tasted), and who now feels alienated from the national Church into which she was ordained.

3. *Affiliation* is the process of a group or individual without previous religious commitment becoming involved with a religious community – sometimes giving rise to allegations of brainwashing.

    There are no brainwashes in this book, but Warnke, Bash, Foster and Harris were fairly theologically virginal when they were captured by the communities from which they eventually escaped.

4. *Intensification* is used to refer to renewed commitment within an existing previous religious affiliation, a deepening of commitment or marking something central to life which was previously peripheral.

    It might be said that, since we have selected as contributors those who have made significant moves from their original faith communities, by definition no contributor falls into this class. But life is not so neat. 'I feel that in some ways, even though I left the Catholic Church, I did not cease being a Catholic', writes Bohache. It's a widely and deeply repercussive observation. Is Catholicism (or any other creed) to do with the ability to recite a catechism? Is one's Catholic identity determined by the view of other Catholics? (and if so which other Catholics?), or by oneself? Are we the only – or at least the predominant – arbiters of our own identity? Is theological authenticity the ability to align oneself unreservedly with the canons of the church? Or is it rather to align oneself unreservedly with oneself, and to feel no dissonance between the convictions perceived as constitutive of oneself and those that one perceives as central to the relevant faith group? If the latter, Bohache is perhaps still a Catholic. For him 'good theology, good ethics and good ecclesiology should be engaged in the pursuit of authentic personhood for all of God's creatures', and he seems not to have abandoned the hope that that's the pursuit of genuine Catholicism too.

5. *Apostasy* refers to a rejection of and defection from a previous religious group or orientation which leads to the adoption of a new or prior religious system or of non-religious beliefs or values. The processes involved in leaving a group are important in the study of personal change. There has been particular scholarly focus on forced 'deprogramming' and defection from New Religious Movements.

    Each of these types involves different degrees of change and different processes. Some require a major reconstitution of a belief system and traumatic social dislocation: others demand only a minimal degree of social or institutional movement.

Conclusion

Our main concern in this volume has been with apostasy, but it would be naïve and wrong to ignore the disruptions that take place in intensification, transition and affiliation. And, as we have already observed, apostasy may be in the eye of the beholder. A journey from X to Y may be perceived by the traveller to be a journey from apostasy to orthodoxy, or into greater orthodoxy, yet by the community left behind as diabolical apostasy. In this book, Baxter doesn't see himself as an apostate at all, but as a convert to Christianity. His Catholic family disagreed, and perhaps still do. Few of St Augustine's former friends begrudged his new-found faith, but John Henry Newman's conversion from Anglicanism to Roman Catholicism was seen by many as betrayal: some of his dearest friends and colleagues never spoke with him again. Whatever it is, apostasy does not merely involve a change of mind. It involves a change of friends, fellowship and one's relationship with physical and temporal spaces. Abandoning a beloved church building or accommodating to a new liturgical calendar can be traumatic. It may involve loss of family, or a radically altered relationship with family. Apostasy may be as painful as separation and divorce – for both parties – and it may take decades to recover and restore previous relationships – if indeed recovery occurs at all. Sometimes apostasy is seen as death, and is followed by a bereavement reaction for all parties.

Some scholars theorise that conversion in the contemporary western world is partly the product of particular social, cultural or psychological contexts. One of these contexts may be a sense of crisis, in which religion offers a new coherent pattern of organisation and meaning for the convert or 'apostate' and makes better sense of the world than any social, therapeutic or psychological alternatives.

There are good reasons for religious people to understand conversion in this revolutionary way, rather than in the more adaptive and mellow way that the term is often used in secular contexts. Consider, for example, Paul the Apostle – one of the first and most dramatic converts to Christianity. The Book of Acts records that Saul (his pre-Christian name) was a zealous persecutor of Christians. But on the road to Damascus he had a dramatic encounter. He saw a bright light, which made him temporarily blind, and heard the voice of Jesus. He emerged from his blindness as a convert to a new faith – or at least to a radically new way of seeing and practising Judaism. Paul's 'Damascus Road experience' (a common phrase that has entered English idiom) is a typical trope for what many regard as religious conversion: 'I once was blind, but now I see', is how one hymn writer puts it.

His conversion made Paul a scandalous, offensive apostate in the eyes of many. But drama, scandal and immediate offence are not necessarily of the essence of apostasy. There is indeed plenty of drama in the New Testament conversion stories: the Christian Church dates its birth from the feast of Pentecost, a truly dramatic occasion, where the disciples received the Holy Spirit. But the rupture with the old ways did not at first seem as significant as it later proved to be: At the end of the gospels, the followers of Jesus were still Jewish, even if, like their master, they were out of sorts with the Pharisees and Sadducees. Many Christians in the years that followed continued to see themselves as Jewish.

Although it made some tectonic theological claims and personal demands, Christianity was a pragmatic and accommodating religion almost from the very beginning. Conversion took many forms. Christian missionaries, as they began to spread throughout Europe and towards India, discovered that where the more familiar elements of a culture were retained, there was likely to be more success in introducing the 'new' religion. For example, Rodney Stark points out that 'by thinly overlaying pagan festivals and sacred places with Christian interpretations, the [seventh-century] missionaries made it easier [for people] to become Christian – so easy that actual conversion seldom occurred.' With the adoption of a new creed, the seeds of heterodoxy and apostasy were sown. Unless there is a fixed point, one cannot deviate.

It was psychologically and politically shrewd for the missionaries to seek to baptise the existing practices, rather than demand their abolition. As an evangelistic strategy it often appealed to the rulers – who may have found the theological claims of Christianity more alluring than did their people. But it did not always work. It was sometimes politically impossible. Stark cites the example of the pagan king, Clovis, who, though baptised as a Christian, would not forsake his ancestral gods: 'The people that followeth me will not suffer that I forsake their gods', he declared. The early European monastically-based missionaries normally worked on the wives of kings, princes and rulers, converting them to Christianity first. Although Christianity gradually 'trickled down', sometimes over hundreds of years, from the elite converts to the masses (Iwerne had plenty of historical precedent), elements of paganism survived.

It was no different for the European missionaries who set out in the nineteenth and twentieth centuries. Faced with practices that appeared not to correspond with ordinary enculturated westernised Christian values, missionaries often had to adapt their message and praxis to secure conversions. Vincent Donovan was a missionary amongst the Masai of East Africa. In his moving account of his work, Donovan describes how his own account of the Christian faith was profoundly challenged. There were high linguistic, cultural and conceptual barriers.

The Masai, for instance, insisted that the whole tribe had to be baptised. It was all or none. They were offended by the idea that individuals could be included or excluded from the rite. Once the tribe was baptised, the tribal baptism was seen as a radical *fulfilment* of the gospel. The tribal elder, Ndnagoya, explained that the catechesis became part of the culture: the lazy were helped by those with energy, the stupid were supported by the intelligent, and those with faith aided those who had little. The tribe could truly say 'we believe'.

This was just one of many epiphanies for Donovan. Is this view of catechesis orthodoxy, heterodoxy, doctrinal deviance, or even a form of apostasy? Donovan simply notes his own conversion – a journey from spiritual individualism to baptismal communitarianism.

Apostasy and conversion cannot have precise meanings, save to signify that someone now belongs to a new faith in a new way, or perhaps an old faith in a way perceived by them and/or others as radically new, and renounces their former beliefs. In saying 'beliefs' in this imprecise formulation we note that there is no clear distinction between belief and praxis. Belief may generate or be generated by praxis; praxis may *be* belief.

Most of the world's major religions begin with their founders being 'converted', or making a radical new claim about themselves and their authority, and consequently being driven out. We note that Jesus himself is an archetypal apostate: a scandal both to the Sadducees (the Temple hierarchy) and the Pharisees (themselves seen as heterodox by the Sadducees). Jesus is an apostate 'stumbling block' who claimed that he had come to 'fulfil' the law and the prophets, but in his ministry so radicalised the reading and understanding of the Jewish faith that

Conclusion

his followers eventually 'converted', – at least in the eyes of the Jewish mainstream, and albeit through a series of encounters and a progressive evolution of belief and practice.

At the beginning of the third millennium, conversion remains an important issue for churches, and also for non-Christian faiths. In the case of Christianity, many mainstream denominations focus on evangelisation, re-evangelisation and Christian education as never before. With society increasingly moulded by more secular values, and with generations now being raised that have 'gospel amnesia,' the task of conversion has become more demanding, and demands more imagination. Christian knowledge can no longer be assumed. Correspondingly, many patterns of evangelism once avidly practised by churches are now being discarded in favour of more long-term programmes that seek to impart religious knowledge and Christian education within the public sphere. Often this is done through schools and other public institutions, and also occurs where the church is responsible for marking birth, marriage and death. Such activity does not normally result in conversion, but it does begin to recreate the context in which churches might once again be able to talk about tradition, transformation and transcendence with some confidence.

Our focus in this book has not primarily been on conversion to a faith from no-faith, but on movement within Christianity (though not all our contributors have seen their journey that way), and on the experiences and perceptions of the voyagers, and the perceptions of those whom they left behind.

We cannot demonstrate that the contributions here are typical experiences of apostasy in the twenty-first century. They no doubt reflect, through the selection of the contributors, our own unconscious biases. We have done our best to triumph over those biases, and have no doubt failed. We suspect, though, that the selection is reasonably representative of 'apostasy' in the western world. Outside Europe and North America apostasy is often a very different matter, and we do not pretend to have captured any of its flavour there.

There is one very striking characteristic common to all our contributors except for Baxter. It is that the move taken by them and/or by others to constitute apostasy has been in the direction of decreased adherence to a set of catechismal propositions; in the direction of increased questioning and fewer certainties. That, at first blush, is a direction of travel opposite to that of many of the apostates of old, who often apostatised because, in their new faith, they found new certainty.

On reflection, though, we wonder if modern (or post-modern) apostasy is really so different from the old. Yes, the whole post-modern zeitgeist ostensibly frowns on definite declarations, but has made uncertainty and the mandate to interrogate one's presumptions pillars of faith as solid and unquestionable as the bodily resurrection was to past generations of the faithful. Perhaps, in expressing this new type of certainty-about-uncertainty, some at least of the 'apostates' in this book are really reciting the new mainstream creed. Perhaps the moves they describe are no different in kind from a move from one view of transubstantiation to another. And there are new certain-certainties, too, which may be held as devoutly as an article in the catechism: belief that gender is fluid, for instance; or that women have as much authority as men to preach; or that revelation is a continuing process, to be discerned with the help of science, archaeology and intuition; or that the core business of religion is authentic personhood.

Uncomfortable though it is, we must finally observe that we found it difficult to find contributors who have moved from a definite, considered 'high church' faith to a 'low church' faith.

Conclusion

We tried hard. There are, of course, many disillusioned cradle-Catholics (for example) who have found a home in (for instance) evangelical Protestantism, but whenever we have examined such cases we have seen a reaction not against Catholic theology, but against nominalism and/or culture. It is interesting to note, again, that Baxter sees his conversion not as a conversion from Catholicism to Protestantism, but from unbelief to Christianity.

Full exploration of this observation (in relation to which there are surely countless counter-examples) is well beyond the scope of this book. But if there is any truth in it, the reasons may lie in pervasive (and some would say corrosive) post-modernity; or in the success of Enlightenment scepticism; or in the human appetite for mystery; or in a distrust of the sort of propositions that can be framed in language – along the lines of 'The Tao that can be spoken is not the eternal Tao'.

What has 'apostasy' done to our contributors? Many things, not easily summarised. In each case there has been a cost to the 'apostate' and others. There have been fractures within the family; hurt, rejection, tension and misunderstanding. There has also been a perhaps surprising amount of healing and rehabilitation. Perhaps that has something to do with a rising secular culture of tolerance. But in each case, too, there is a palpable sense, on the part of the 'apostate', of relief. They can now spread their wings. They can be themselves in a way they could not before. Perhaps Bohache is right about the centrality in religion of personal authenticity.

No contributor looks wistfully back over their shoulder, wishing they could go back. Except possibly in the cases of Harris and Foster (whose betrayal of the Iwerne ethos means that they would be blackballed if they re-applied for club membership), there is no obvious reason why, so far as the original constituency is concerned, they could not return. Perhaps some do creep into

163

the back of their old churches from time to time, perhaps to reassure themselves that they made the right decision to leave, or to recalibrate the bench marks that allow them to assess their own direction and speed or travel, or just out of love or sentiment. If they're recognised, they'll probably be given a cup of coffee or a hug. At the worst they'll be given a hard glance and a cold shoulder.

Whatever it is, apostasy is not what it was in the bad old days.

Study Guide for Groups

These case studies make challenging reading. We think that apostasy is not what it used to be, and has now morphed into a coded way for describing a person defecting from a tribe to some other (usually broader, larger) form of faith. We realise this is a value judgment on our part. However, if your Study Group, Chaplaincy Seminar Discussion or Book Club wants to pursue the themes and ideas further, we have some suggestions on how to frame the kinds of conversations that might be fruitful. If nothing else, the case studies are helpful for prompting some self-critical reflection, and interrogating some of our own prejudices.

A fundamental starting point is to acknowledge that we cannot understand others unless we listen. Deep listening comes before deep literacy — the capacity to comprehend others. We begin with tenderness, humility and kindness, so that we constantly recognise there is always 'someone other than me' to be accommodated. If we don't make space for them in our conversations, deliberations and society, many will feel that they are never heard.

Those who are snubbed, patronised, oppressed or marginalised because of their sexuality, ethnicity or class will also raise their voices in pain and protest. Tender listening is not just a form of pastoral care. Done properly, with integrity, it is one of the first stages in political action. After all, if you are not going to be changed yourself as a result of listening to the pain and alienation of others, and are not prepared to work to change their world, why would you bother giving them the time of day in the first place? When you listen, ask yourself, 'What am I going to do for this person or this group, as a result of hearing them and feeling their pain?'

Your group discussion might find this exercise hard, but it can be helpful to imagine, and even role play, what it is like for the religious group, sect or tribal kraal to lose someone to another expression of Christian faith. It is worth trying to contemplate their fears and fantasies, and perhaps attempting to walk in their shoes.

Jeanette Winterson's *Oranges Are Not the Only Fruit* (Pandora Press, 1985) is a short semi-autobiographical book that can provide an excellent starting point for reflecting on the dynamics of constraint and freedom, loss and gain, together with the ambiguity of apostasy. It is also a coming-of-age book that skilfully navigates sexuality, sexual awakening and belonging in a small Pentecostal church. The book was adapted into BAFTA-winning 1990 BBC TV drama of the same name.

Winterson's story concerns a lesbian girl called Jeanette who has been adopted by a working class couple who are evangelists in the Elim Pentecostal Church. The book covers transitions from youth to adulthood, complex family relationships, the stigma imposed by organised religion on same-sex relations, and the concept of faith.

Jeanette grows up in a gritty town in northern England (Accrington, Lancashire), believing she is destined and called to be a missionary. However, as an adolescent, Jeanette finds herself attracted to another girl, and upon discovering this, the religious friends of the couple subject Jeanette and her friend to a sustained programme of exorcisms.

We also warmly commend Denise Cottrell-Boyce's *Welcoming the Stranger* (Darton, Longman and Todd, 2021). This is one of the books from the publisher's 'How the Bible Can Help Us Understand' series. The books use novels, personal stories, suggestions for individual and group reflections, and of course, portions of scripture. The books take an angular look at issues, and are likely to appeal to groups that foster exploration and welcome curiosity.

You might also try engaging at the same time with a non-religious text. We recommend Malcolm Gladwell's *Talking to Strangers* (Penguin, 2020), subtitled as 'What we should know about the people we don't know'. You might also give some thought to reading around the topic of listening. What does it mean to really tune in to another person's life? How can we enter into the experience of others? On one level, we can't. But we can learn to lay the foundations for empathy, deep sympathy and, ultimately, compassion, and therefore increase our ability to enter into the lives of others.

Kathryn Mannix's *Listen: How to Find the Words for Tender Conversations* (Collins, 2021) is a good introduction for individuals and groups. Why do we avoid difficult conversations? Why do we not mention the elephant in the room? Why do we tend to skirt around what matters most? Mannix sees tenderness and kindness as being key to listening. We cannot speak our hearts and minds (though we love to do so!) until we have learned truly to hear others.

Discussion groups could begin with taking a chapter a week from Jessica Nordell's *The End of Bias: How We Change Our Minds* (Granta Publications, 2021) or Jennifer L. Eberhardt's *Biased: Uncovering the Hidden Prejudices That Shape Our Lives* (Random House, 2019). Both authors explore unintentional bias and the persistent prejudices that often clash with our more consciously held beliefs. Nordell writes with warmth and humour, and is prepared to take on subjects such as the prevalence of diversity training courses in organisations, and why they often fall short.

Most good education, together with decent theology, quite a lot of spirituality, and certainly nearly all faith development, is conversational in character. We learn as we listen, and is often changed when we truly hear. We also listen when we speak, as we come to put words to our experiences. We discover their partiality and how provisional they are. So we come to listen in a spirit of humility, being humble even to ourselves. Some things that might seem apostasy to some are cherished as treasure by others.

If you are minded to use this book as a basis for discussions, we recommend that you set some ground rules for listening and speaking with one another. It is far too easy in group dynamics to fall into unhelpful binaries like listener-speaker and leader-led. We suggest that you take a different approach, and try to inhabit the beliefs and worldview of others from the outset.

For example, you might like to have a discussion about how your beliefs and values on sexuality and religion have changed – or stayed the same – over the course of your life. Have you always thought what you now think? Were there any experiences, meetings or people from the past that began to change or intensify the way you believed? When did you last hear a sermon on this subject? How did it make you feel? And what did it make you think?

Then, rather than tell the group all of this, spend no more than five minutes summarising it to the person sitting nearest you. We suggest the following rules: You cannot be interrupted in those five minutes. Your partner may make notes and may ask questions for clarification for no more than two minutes at the end. Then reverse roles. Having both made notes, and the rest of the group likewise, your partner then speaks for you for around three minutes, summarising what they (hopefully!) have heard.

Their summary should be positive, fair and not subjected to

any qualifying comments or criticism. The presentation of your beliefs and experiences should be undertaken by your partner *at least* as an advocate or attorney might for a defendant in a case. Ideally, however, they would speak not just for you, but *as* you – in role, occupying and owning your beliefs and values, and done as though this is all that matters. All in the group should do likewise for the other, as an act of generous hospitality.

Having listened to one another, one person can take responsibility for moderating a discussion and drawing the common threads together. But the group should also carefully note the areas that have seemed peripheral, and which perhaps only one person mentioned or touched on. The group can then reflect, later, on how discussion of these experiences and beliefs might be taken forward.

Proceeding in this way will enable the group to develop respectful, empathetic and possibly compassionate modes of listening, modes unlikely to develop if we find ourselves pressed in self-defence over our beliefs and values. This can be a difficult process, to be sure. But trust it and stay with it, and with one another. We cannot understand others unless we take these kinds of steps.

Listening and speaking like this can help us begin to own what it is like to be the 'other person' – someone else – with their life, beliefs and experiences, and the pleasure and rewards, or the pain and stigma, that these may bring.

Some beliefs are a liberating gift; others can be an oppressive burden. Remember that most people who hold sincere beliefs don't think that they chose them, as though on a shopping spree. Many people think that their beliefs chose them. They don't hold beliefs; they are held *by* them.

The case studies in this short book would make for a reasonable discussion of around sixty to seventy-five minutes over four to six weeks or so. Below we offer a few ideas to help get you started in discussions.

1. Some of our previously held beliefs were (literally) infantile (e.g., in the Tooth Fairy). What was it like to lose those beliefs? How do we respond to adults whom we suppose still hold infantile beliefs?

2. Beliefs live side by side with values. What values and beliefs did you grow up with, and how did you come to be a moral, spiritual being?

3. When you lost a belief (e.g., in the Tooth Fairy,) did you feel any anger or sense of betrayal for having been pressed to participate in a realm of belief you now know to be wrong?

4. Are there any aspects of your faith tradition to which you sit light, or prefer not to believe at all? How do you relate to people in your faith tradition who strongly hold on to and stand by these beliefs?

5. Sometimes the experiences and encounters we have can confound and transform us, leaving us radically changed. Can you describe a moment or season that has changed the way you think, believe and live?

6. The thing about other people is that we never really understand how they tick until we get to know them better. How has a relationship with some 'other' altered the way you see them, and yourself?

7. Wisdom often surfaces when we least expect it, and from

sources that we would not normally have chosen. How has your landscape of belief been shaped by the insights of others?

We recommend several films and television series as sources for reflection – for instance the 'indie' film *Blue Like Jazz* (2012), based on the semi-autobiographical sketches penned by Donald Miller (Nelson, 2003). *Blue Like Jazz* tracks the journey of a young man who, from an evangelical upbringing where higher education could only mean going to Bible College, stumbles into being a student at a liberal arts college.

Dubbed 'non-religious thoughts on Christian spirituality', the central character finds profound theological resonance in jazz greats such as John Coltrane and Miles Davis. The film is a compelling narrative of one young man's battle with his fear of being labelled apostate, yet who nonetheless finds a very profound faith in God as the film closes.

More recently, the Channel 4 television series sitcom *Everyone Else Burns* (2023) charts, in six episodes, the trials and tribulations of a Pentecostal Manchester-based family as they make ready for the end of the world. This is, of course, a world in which they as the redeemed will be saved, and everyone else will burn.

The series is touching and tender in its handling of religion, and also very, very funny. The wit is caustically sharp at times, and manages to expose hyper-religiosity (and the self-regard of the witty protagonists), yet in a way that illuminates empathetically the minutiae of family dynamics. As an insider-account – a kind of apologia – the series gives the viewer valuable insights into apostasy, yet without mocking the faith that chooses to regard former members as apostate.

These are a few suggestions for group discussion. Give them a try and see how you get on. If you can walk even a few paces in somebody else's shoes, you might begin to understand their life and journey. Most importantly, try to see the case studies from all sides. What was it like for that person to leave? What was it like to be left? Who bore the costs? What bridges or paths back were left? Why does leaving a faith feel like a bereavement, or divorce, or worse? When, if at all, do the bereft recover? How do people live with the stigma of being dubbed 'apostate'?

When you have discussed these questions, and perhaps some others of your own, one remains. How then shall we live?